Advance Praise for *Getting Along with Rusty*

"Sharing one's personal experiences of growth and reflection is such an important part of our healing journey. In a very powerful and accessible way, Bartlett does just this as a human being, a trauma practitioner, and an equine therapist in *Getting Along with Rusty*. I encourage others to read her story as part of their healing."
—*Dave Berger, MFT, PT, LCMHC, Senior International Somatic Experiencing® Faculty*

"*Getting Along with Rusty* is a must-read by anyone who has ever experienced Developmental Trauma or felt themselves resistant to the advice of their parents or others. Bartlett weaves a compelling story about her personal journey through healing, and how a most unexpected healing partner, Rusty, taught her about love and safety on the deepest of levels. Rusty opens all our eyes to the probability of healing through a relationship of love and support, through connecting with equines to shed the layers of trauma we acquire during our life. This book is more than a good read; it has the potential to change lives."
—*Stephen J. Terrell, PsyD, Co-author of* Nurturing Resilience: Helping Clients Move Forward from Developmental Trauma

"Everyone working with horses and therapy needs to read *Getting Along with Rusty*, really. But it is also for anyone who understands the gifts inherent in the human/horse relationship and how they help us grow into fully-formed humans. Bartlett shares with honesty and clarity her personal journey of learning through horses, and along the way offers insight and guidance on how we can help the horses we love be happier and healthier. Many of us feel

the dissonance between our love for these amazing creatures and how it is considered normal for us to dominate and exploit them. Bartlett offers a different point of view, and an opportunity to work towards a more equitable relationship. It starts with us."
—Nayana Morag, founder of Essential Animals, and author of Essential Oils for Animals

"Bartlett does an amazing job of combining stories of her personal journey with horses, with tangible exercises that can benefit anyone in the horse world. Her love of horses and passion for equine well-being shine through every word as she takes the reader through her life with Rusty, her encounters with other horses and horse people, and the recognition of how these fit into the equine-assisted world. In addition to her compassion for the equine, Bartlett weaves in lessons for the rest of us, for both personal growth and how to be better for our horses. This is a truly remarkable tale with lessons for all of us."
—Emily Kieson, PhD, MS, PGDip, Executive Director, Equine International

"Trauma can show up in any room or round pen. Understanding the impacts of adversity in humans and in equines, and what can unfold when we are in relationship with these creatures, offers the opportunity to move into greater safety and connection with one another. Bartlett offers a beautiful mix of personal anecdotes and education to inform the reader about the nervous system and the conditions required to help it to renegotiate trauma, with details that are beneficial for multiple species. A vulnerable, relatable, and hopeful read that reminds us that every moment yields opportunities for something to be different and for healing to occur, for two- and four-legged friends."
—Sarah Schlote, MA, RP, CCC, SEP, founder of EQUUSOMA® Horse-Human Trauma Recovery

Getting Along with Rusty

HORSES, HEALING,
AND THERAPEUTIC RIDING
(Mostly a Memoir)

Lasell Jaretzki Bartlett, MSW

LILITH HOUSE PRESS
ESTES PARK, COLORADO

Copyright © 2023 by Lasell Jaretzki Bartlett. All rights reserved. No part of this book, except for brief review, may be reproduced, stored in a retrieval system, or transmitted in any form or by other means—electronic, mechanical, photocopying, recording, or otherwise—without the written permission of the copyright owner. For information, contact the author: lasellbartlettauthor@gmail.com.

Cover and book design by Gopa & Ted2, Inc.
Ebook design by Jane Dixon-Smith
Cover photo © Jennifer Judkins Godin
Author photograph © Ange DiBenedetto

"Protocol for Falls" adapted from *Trauma Through a Child's Eye: Awakening the Ordinary Miracle of Healing*, by Peter A. Levine and Maggie Kline, published by North Atlantic Books, copyright © 2007, 2019 by Peter A. Levine and Maggie Kline. Reprinted with permission of North Atlantic Books.

"That Saturday" adapted from *What She Wrote: An Anthology of Women's Voices*, published by Lilith House Press, copyright © 2020 by Lilith House Press and Lasell Jaretzki Bartlett. Reprinted with permission.

Disclaimer of liability: This book is a memoir. It reflects the author's present recollections of experiences over time. The events and conversations in this book have been set down to the best of the author's ability. While the book is as accurate as the author can make it, there may be errors, omissions, and inaccuracies. To protect the privacy of individuals, names and identifying details have been changed, composite characters have been created, locations have been altered or left unspecified, and dialogue has been recreated. The contents and information in this book are for informational use only and are not intended to be a substitute for professional advice. The author shall have neither liability nor responsibility to any person or entity with respect to any loss or damage caused or alleged to be caused directly or indirectly by the information contained in this book.

First Printing
ISBN 979-8-9858101-5-8 (hardcover)
ISBN 979-8-9858101-4-1 (softcover)
ISBN 979-8-9858101-6-5 (ebook)
Library of Congress Control Number: 2023908972
Bartlett, Lasell Jaretzki
Getting along with Rusty: horses, healing, and therapeutic riding
(mostly a memoir)

Published by Lilith House Press
www.lilithhousepress.org • www.lasellbartlett.com

Keywords: Memoir | Self-help | Horses | Therapeutic riding | Healing with horses | Trauma | Developmental trauma

It's our responsibility to show the horses how to fit in our world.
HARRY WHITNEY

Table of Contents

Part One: Foundations

Prologue — 3
Love at First Sight — 3
Hope — 6

Chapter 1: Beginnings — 9
Early-Onset Horse Crazy — 9
The First Lesson — 10
My Copper Penny — 11
Beginnings — 15

Chapter 2: Entering the Profession — 17
Hello, Therapeutic Riding — 17
In Service to the Vulnerable Ones — 18
Time for Changes — 21
Teaching and Differences — 24
Entering — 26

Part Two: Survival 101

Chapter 3: Safe, Fearful, and Beyond — 31
Am I Safe with You? — 31
Pause Button — 35

    Safe, Fearful, and Beyond: Autonomic Nervous
        System Basics   38

CHAPTER 4: Feeling Safe   41
    Energized and Connected   41
    Can We Give Up the Fight?   43
    He Knows His Job   45
    Newness Again and Again   49
    Feeling Safe   50

CHAPTER 5: When I'm Scared   57
    Fear Takes Over   57
    Bronc Ride Breakthroughs   58
    Ollie and Chip   62
    When I'm Scared   64

CHAPTER 6: Immobilization   67
    Scared and Alone   67
    Bridling Rusty   69
    Hard to Be Here   71
    Recovery Not Guaranteed   75
    Immobilization   77

CHAPTER 7: Emerging from Immobilization   81
    Expecting Too Much   81
    Catching My Breath   83
    Enthusiasm   85
    Emerging from Immobilization   87

PART THREE: PROGRESS, NOT PERFECTION

CHAPTER 8: Boundaries   95
    Don't Tell Me What to Do   95
    That Far Away   96

TABLE OF CONTENTS

This Much Space — 99
Boundaries — 103

CHAPTER 9: Body Language — 109
My Teacher — 109
Adjusting Plans — 111
Conflict in Action — 114
Body Language — 116

CHAPTER 10: Communication — 121
Trailer Terror — 121
Humming — 125
Communication — 127

CHAPTER 11: Learning — 133
At the Scratching Cone — 133
I'm Learning — 135
Distrust and Belief — 137
The Tank Challenge — 138
Learning — 140

CHAPTER 12: Paying Attention — 145
Winter Practice — 145
What Is It? — 146
Hurry to Here — 147
Practicing Softness — 150
Learning to Soften — 151
Manley's Treatment Plan — 154
Paying Attention — 156

CHAPTER 13: Pressure — 159
The Pushy One — 159
Bracing — 162
Ruby's Treatment Plan — 165

Don't Hurry Me!	166
Pressure	170
CHAPTER 14: Falls and Co-regulation	175
Getting Together with Rusty	175
Self-Propelled	176
Will You Catch Me?	178
First Aid for Falls	179
Falls and Co-regulation	179

PART FOUR: ESPECIALLY THIS

CHAPTER 15: Transitions	185
That Saturday	185
With This Chemo	188
Sudden Loss	190
Transitions	192
CHAPTER 16: Listening	197
Sharing Decisions	197
My Nay Vote	199
Is Anyone Listening?	202
The Simple Cure	205
Listening	208
CHAPTER 17: Be the Calm	211
Am I Ready to Ride?	211
Singing	213
Falling Off	215
Be the Calm	218
EPILOGUE	221
Fixing the Gutter	221
Dear Rusty	223

SAMPLE EXERCISES	227
Rocking to Balance	227
Story Time	228
Feeling Our Boundaries	229
GRATITUDE	231
PATH INTERNATIONAL	233
Mission Statement	233
Vision Statement	234
REFERENCES	235
ABOUT THE AUTHOR	239

Part One:
Foundations

Prologue

I always say without hope, you won't take action, because if you don't believe that your action is going to be useful, why would you bother? — JANE GOODALL

LOVE AT FIRST SIGHT

RUSTY WAS SIX months old and living in solitary confinement when we first met. Although five other horses were in the barn, the windowless box stall with floor-to-ceiling walls prevented him from seeing or touching them. This was where he was born and this was where he lived with his mother for three months before she was moved from the barn, leaving him behind.

I could barely see his face, dark against the background of his unlit stall. Light from the opened barn door glinted off his wide eyes. He strained to reach over the stall door, curious, seeking to interact, yearning for contact. My heart broke open then and there, despite my knowing nothing about how much this young horse's psyche was already broken.

I had gone to this farm searching for the history of my recently purchased mare, Kacee. She was a purebred Morgan horse, as my first horse had been decades earlier. When I bought Kacee, I had been told I could get her registration papers from her breeders. Through a network of local horsey folks, I found her breeders, Bert and Linda Molsen, and arranged to meet them. There I also met four of Kacee's nieces and nephews, the foals born that year:

Reflection, Replica, Rhapsody, and Rusty. That was 1997, the "Year of Rs." Kacee had been born the "Year of Ks."

I started visiting the farm every few weeks. I offered to spend time with the four foals, thinking I could help socialize and halter train them. Linda was busy with cancer treatments, and Bert was busy worrying about Linda. The foals were stall-bound and needed attention. The Molsens loved their horses but couldn't prioritize the needs of these youngsters for movement and space and contact with other horses.

It was a hot August afternoon when I next visited the Molsens. Linda was in bed recovering from her latest round of chemotherapy. Bert was on his tractor, mowing the small field between the house and the drive. After waving and making eye contact with him, I rolled open the barn doors and stepped inside. I was met by the usual line of yearling faces greeting me from over their stall doors.

Except Rusty's face was missing.

My stomach clenched as I crossed the distance in four strides and stood on my tiptoes so I could see over his stall door. I saw feet—four feet sticking up in the air while the rest of his body lay immobile. He was stuck upside down in the middle of his stall. I turned and rushed to the barn door, starting to yell and wave my arms as I emerged into the sun.

"Bert! Bert! Something's wrong!" Even though Burt couldn't hear my screams, he saw me and turned off the tractor. *"Rusty's upside down!"*

I headed back into the barn and Bert caught up as I opened Rusty's stall door. I held my breath, hearing the sound of Bert's heavy breathing from running, and looking to see if Rusty was breathing and why he wasn't moving. Rusty's eyes were dull and half-closed, and he was breathing. Just as Bert mumbled something about *cast in the damned trough*, I saw that Rusty's spine was nestled in the concrete trough that runs along the floor through all the stalls in the barn. The trough was a remnant of an old cow-barn design with a mechanized system for moving manure out of the stalls. The metal parts were long gone but the trough remained, and it was the perfect size for catching a horse mid-roll and holding him there: a death trap for a large mammal. Rusty had rolled into the trough and was cast, stuck in a position where he couldn't get his feet in place to help himself stand up. He had succumbed into a collapsed state in which the breathing slows, the heart rate slows, and the body is still—conserving energy and perhaps appearing dead to any predators in the area that might otherwise enjoy an easy meal.

Bert gathered the long, thick rope hanging near the ladder to the loft and flung it over one of the barn beams that supported the massive hayloft above the stalls. He dragged one end of the rope to where Rusty lay, wrapping it several times around Rusty's front feet, and then stepped back and started pulling the other end of the rope, slowly tilting Rusty's body to the side. Bert was sweating with effort. I was sweating with fear that Rusty was broken, injured beyond repair. I'd been thinking about buying this little horse and taking him home. I could save him, free him from his stall, while also providing a companion for Kacee. (I had no idea what a challenge this would become.) It was an enticing fantasy. And Rusty was cute. But now maybe he was broken. Maybe it was too late to save him.

As Bert pulled, Rusty was tipped onto his side and started to struggle. His urge to right himself and regain his four-footed stance took over. Bert loosened the rope. Rusty struggled more and got to his feet. He stood there, looking just as stunned right-side up as he had when he was upside down.

This incident clinched it for me. It cemented the heart bond, that connection that can arise when we help save a vulnerable being. I decided to buy him despite his age, despite his being untrained, despite his price tag. My emotions steered the decision, flouting any logical assessment of what I needed in my life. So, I brought Rusty into my life. I now owned a yearling—and I had no experience with young horses.

Rusty is still as curious and eager to interact as he was then. And he sometimes still stands as if confined in that stall with no options ... often just before he explodes into a few bucks and canters off. Horses are not designed to live with limited movement, or separation from their herd. He may always be awkward in his body despite my efforts to help him. I may always be awkward in my body, too, despite my efforts to help myself. Our stories are different and the same. Life events interrupted normal developmental timelines for each of us. People have helped—lots and lots of people offering lots and lots of help. My love for this horse has kept me connected through these years of striving, hopes, injuries, disappointments, and delights.

Hope

Hope. Belief. Faith. Concepts that help us take the next step when each foot is immersed in a five-gallon bucket of wet sand.

Horses are powerful, with untameable souls, mesmerizing to observe in the wild. We love them. In our fenced fields, they do their best to get along despite conditions of confinement. We are only partially aware of how their natural urges are thwarted by living with us. Our eyes are clouded by *equine-ism*—those prejudices arising because we are seldom able to see or name what's happening within the skin of these remarkable animals. We're blinded by our need for what they represent, by our dreamy illusions of what they are. Their stoicism colludes with our blinders. They get enough from us to survive, usually, but what is happening there under that dazzling layer of heartwarming beauty? What are we doing that contributes to the dulled eyes, the tight jaws, the chronic ulcers? What are we doing that contributes to the curiosity, the soft nickers, the readiness to go on an adventure?

I have a long history of not listening to what my father had to say, and I spent many of my younger years doing exactly what he told me not to do. Two big examples: "Do not ride a motorcycle." And, "I forbid you to hitchhike."

Perhaps without his disapproval—his adamant disapproval—I may never have pursued those two high-risk activities. But he disapproved and I was compelled to act. Despite some mishaps, I survived many adventures—like the summer I was twenty-one, hitchhiking on a whim from Ireland, where I was visiting a college friend, to Greece, where I took delight in the turquoise water surrounding pristine islands. Later I learned to ride a dirt bike on an ice-covered road in upstate New York. I never got hurt—but now, at this point in my life, I tend to pause, reflect, and make other choices, safer choices.

As I aged, and maybe as my father aged, we became friendlier and more relaxed together. We each sought help in psychotherapy. He shared his regrets about holding back affection when I was young. He had been trying to please my mother who worried about father and daughter relationships due to her own memories. Dad and I learned to approach our differences with kindness—I had followed many interests and many jobs, whereas he had focused on one profession since his teens. I no longer feared his criticism nor held back on any impulse to hug him, my father.

We were in his living room recovering after Thanksgiving dinner, in 2009, discussing horses and my work as a therapeutic riding instructor. He told me to write a book. I was deeply moved and started this book that evening, responding to my father's approval and encouragement with an outburst of creative energy.

I wanted to help therapy horses be successful and content in their work. Little had been written about the job burnout these horses experience. Initially titled *Enhancing Wellness to Prevent Burnout in Our Therapy Horses*, this was to be a how-to book offering educational ideas and experiential exercises to the professionals and volunteers who work directly with horses in the therapeutic riding profession. It's morphed into this book of my memoirs and essays, as well as a few directions for DIY experiential activities that help people become more aware of and responsive to their horses' needs—or indeed the needs of anybody in their lives. Rusty has been inspiring me—indeed requiring me—to become a better human and a better horse person.

This book begins with the horse experiences that shaped my

relationships and ignited my urge to learn more. My first riding lesson. My first horse. Then some other firsts. My first time volunteering in a therapeutic riding program, and stories from when I worked as a therapeutic riding instructor. Much of my focus lay in introducing and restoring conscious boundaries, conscious balance, and conscious communication. My interest grew in training the staff and volunteers who could in turn attend to meeting a therapy horse's complex needs during a lesson. Those trainings were intended to add to everyone's existing knowledge base about the full scope of a horse's need for clear boundaries and consistent guidance, while increasing everyone's ability to communicate requests from a place of listening, softness, and confidence.

Feeling a sense of safety, connection, and belonging are the foundation blocks of hope. If horses need hope, we are the holders and molders of their access as long as we keep them in domestication.

Understanding and handling horses for what they are—horses, not humans—is not magic, but it does require a change in us: how we think, what we expect, and how we behave. I had to be shown this in person before I could even imagine the possibilities. We *can* change our habits and expectations. Who wouldn't make intense, life-changing efforts as a *gift* to our horses? It is *not* easy, but it's doable.

What has been offered to me, I'd like to pass along to others, in both my life's work and this book: the chance to build self-awareness, to more easily access the present moment devoid of defenses and projections, and to support and relate with our horse friends. There are many, many books, videos, podcasts, webinars, and clinics available to help us learn about horses and their physical, emotional, physiological, and social needs. I encourage you to seek them out. There's no end to what we can learn. I hope this book will be another resource in your healing trajectory. A fuller compilation of DIY experiential exercises will soon be available as a companion book to this. Regarding the people and modalities that have influenced me, I've listed those details on my website: www.lasellbartlett.com.

CHAPTER 1

Beginnings

Let yourself be silently drawn by the strange pull of what you really love. It will not lead you astray. — Rumi

Early-Onset Horse Crazy

I LOVE HORSES. THEY have been my passion since before I can remember. I may not know where the grocery stores and gas stations are, but I know where the horses live, noting each and every one by color and size, and their barns and fields, as I travel through the landscapes of life.

I wrote to Santa each year asking for a pony, my one and only request. I looked through the Sears Roebuck catalog that arrived in the fall for the trained ponies they sold. I figured if my parents could mail order jigsaw puzzles and paint-by-number kits, they could mail order a pony. And if I could have a pony, I would forgo all other gifts. On Christmas morning I covered my disappointment with a smile, reassuring my parents I was pleased, even though there was no pony waiting with a red bow around its neck.

We moved from the suburbs of New York City to a rural region in upstate New York when I was seven, in 1955, and there I started riding lessons. My two teachers, John and Elaine Moffat at the Cooperstown Riding Stables, taught me that a meaningful reward for a horse is to do nothing with them. Don't pat them on the neck and praise them, just be still and quiet. Offer them a pause to mark the special moments. John quickly became a "good father" figure, filling my need for a warm and attentive adult. My parents provided food, shelter, clothing, intellectual stimulation, and access to sports activities. But their anxieties and various life commitments and confusions interfered with their availability and calm. I needed availability and calm. John Moffat and his lesson horses filled that gap. My best summers were when I was old enough to bicycle the five miles to and from the stables every day to do barn chores, groom the horses, clean tack, take lessons, and go for some wild hacks out through woods and fields.

The First Lesson

"Who's Roulette?" I asked.

"See over there under the tree?" John was pointing across the meadow to a big green tree. There was a dark brown horse standing under it. "That's Roulette, and I think you'll like him. He's gentle and especially patient with children. He's been ridden by a lot of kids like you, just learning to ride."

It was my first afternoon at the Moffats' farm. On my seventh birthday, Mom and Dad had told me they would take me every Saturday for riding lessons. I had cried in anticipation and thankfulness, and now I was about to meet the horse I was going to ride.

John had a rope in one hand and a carrot in the other. He broke the carrot and handed a piece to me.

"Here, you carry this. We'll go catch him together. Walk along beside me . . . see how I carry the carrot in front of me and the rope behind me? Now, Roulette, he won't mind being caught by us, but some horses you need to fool a little. They'll come for food, and then while they're eating you slip the rope around their neck. You watch this time, and next time you come, you can do it while I watch. Okay?" I nodded my head, listening to John while looking at Roulette.

We were halfway across the meadow when Roulette turned his head in response to our approach.

"He sees us coming," I half-squealed, half-whispered, barely able to contain my excitement.

As John and I moved closer, Roulette perked his ears forward, showing interest in our arrival. On a flat, open hand John held out the carrot.

"Hey there, Roulette . . . hey, old boy," he cooed. I was at John's side, attentive because it was important to me. I wanted to be able to do this next week.

We stepped in as Roulette stretched out his neck and nibbled at the carrot. John quietly slipped the rope around Roulette's neck in order to lead him to the barn.

"Now you offer him your carrot. Just remember to let it rest on your open hand. That's it. Keep your fingers straight so he'll eat the carrot and not your fingers."

I felt proud and happy as Roulette ate off the palm of my hand, tickling me with the whiskers on his chin.

John stood silently while I started to make friends with Roulette. "Oh, Roulette, I'm glad to meet you." I stood awed by the big animal. "I hope you'll be good to me while I learn to ride you."

A few moments went by before John spoke. "Okay. Let's walk him in to the barn now."

As John and I took our first steps, Roulette followed alongside. He was familiar with carrots and kids. He was looking forward to the love and care he could expect from me, his new little friend.

My Copper Penny

My father had built stalls in our barn and filled the loft with hay. Then there we were, Dad and me and John Moffat and Phil, the local horse dealer, shopping for my very own horse.

I had a twelve-year-old's short list of criteria for my first horse: one who was trained for English riding and could jump. That was it. I imagine my father and John had their own criteria: They would want a horse that cost less than their maximum price and was healthy and safe for a young girl to handle and ride.

First, I was shown a handsome palomino gelding who fit the bill. But I didn't feel a clear yes and I asked if there were other horses I could meet. Phil pointed to the paddock. My heart skipped a beat and swelled like a balloon when I saw this shiny copper bay standing there watching us. I half-heard "young Morgan" and "ridden Western" and "never jumped anything" over the pounding of my heart. It was love at first sight. My criteria didn't matter. My gut feeling was: *This is the one.* A week later, the four-year-old registered Morgan gelding, My Copper Penny, stepped off the trailer in front of our barn. I had my very own horse.

I knew nothing of the breed. He came with a registration certificate but the names on it were meaningless. We knew nothing about contacting the breed registry to have ownership transferred. (I later got a printout to satisfy my hindsight curiosity. He had some nice old Morgan bloodlines.)

After a few days, I turned him out in the field, which was strung with barbed wire. Dad had set this up, not knowing that barbed wire wasn't safe for horses. I was on the front lawn playing with my younger brothers and looked up to see Penny come trotting toward us. What? How did he get out? After putting him in his stall, I walked the fence line looking carefully for a break. The fence was intact, which meant Penny had jumped over it to come and be close. Here was my new horse with no English training and no history of jumping, but that boy could jump!

We bonded quickly, which (at my age of twelve) probably meant I had fallen in love and he was a lonely, easy-going horse. We went on adventures without a worry, riding on the tree-lined trails from home to neighbors', from home to the Moffats' stables, or sometimes just for walks together side by side up the dirt road that led from our house into the woods and beyond. That first winter I tied baling twine together, making a harness so he could pull me on skis. Our path lit by a winter's full moon, we went out together across the snow into those woods. (I later learned that this is a bona fide sport called skijoring.)

One day, I was riding through the pine woods with a couple of friends from the Cooperstown Stables. We approached a meadow, an expanse of green grass dotted with yellow where the spring dandelions reached for the sun. Our excitement grew as we moved into the open. Three young teenagers, our horses coiling like springs, ready for the race we always made across this field.

"I'll beat you to the gate!" Jamie cried out and we all burst into full gallop. My Morgan was smaller than Jamie's Thoroughbred and Fran's Saddlebred, but that didn't stop Penny and me from winning yet another race. Penny was compact and fit and loved to run.

He was equally content to walk or trot and would proceed on an adventure with me whenever I asked. Penny—the epitome of a willing, responsive horse—set the bar high for future horses I would own. I became familiar with this wondrous feeling of togetherness, even though later in life I didn't know how to bring it out in a horse who wasn't offering it. Decades later, I'm still refining my skills.

I rode in lessons and in local horse shows. I went hacking with other barn rats. But all those accomplishments and adventures were minor compared with how Penny touched my heart.

My first experience of being angry—furious and out-of-control angry—was in the barn with Penny. He wouldn't do something I wanted him to do, although I don't now recall what that was. I started hitting him, on his shoulder, on his neck. Wailing with my voice and flailing with my arms and hands, my whole upper chest tight. I was frantic. And he stood there. He didn't fight back. He didn't run away. He didn't swing his head at me, or bite or kick out at me. It must have been unsettling, but he didn't close off to me in my rage.

He'd hung out with me when I was nice, when I fed him and went on adventures with him—the two of us alone, or together with a bunch of other horses and riders. He was calm. He was ready. He accepted my direction. Then I experienced him accepting strong emotions from me. He saw me in my rawest, most vulnerable state. Like nobody else had seen, maybe ever. He accepted me when I was that upset and out of control.

My mother had raved or perhaps bragged about what a good baby I'd been—never asking for anything, happy to play in my room for hours. But I was not actually happy, or even content. I was shut down—living in a state of shock from the time when, at six months old, I was suffocated when my older brother put a pillow over my face and sat on it. Although my mother noticed in time to save me, she had not been present and aware enough to help me ease out of the shock. I remained shut down until Penny was there for me. He was my first memorable experience of a calm, attentive presence. I felt safe with him. Safe enough to lose it. Safe enough to act out some part of my survival rage. And he witnessed it. No judgment, no defensiveness, no running away. I felt seen. I felt accepted.

This is really hard for me to write. It's difficult to get in touch again with who I was when I was a young teen—isolated, socially lost, and disconnected, living in a family where indoor activity meant all of us sat around the glossy antique wooden dining room table, each playing our own game of solitaire. I got through those years with the help of tobacco and alcohol. Both gave me a sense of belonging with others while helping numb me emotionally to the despair and emptiness and fear I lived with. Nobody—myself included—saw or understood how much I was struggling then.

Penny touched my heart on a daily basis. He wanted to be with me. I wanted to be with him. Then the normal adolescent hormones kicked in, and my attention turned to boys. When it became clear I would be going to boarding school in 1963, I sold my horse. Many years later, in 1991, Penny appeared in a series of dreams that became my *Dream Horse Poems*—published in *What She Wrote: An Anthology of Women's Voices*, Lilith House Press, 2020—bringing to consciousness some of the conflicts, delights, and agonies of those childhood years.

Beginnings

We all begin somewhere. Maybe at conception, maybe before conception. Did I begin when my mother's egg granted entry to my father's sperm? Or did I begin when either of them first dreamed of a second child, perhaps even dared to want a girl child? My love of horses—did it begin with my first longings, or did it begin with my grandparents who owned horses, or perhaps ancestors before them? I know it started long before I met Roulette or Penny.

There were times when I thought I was a hotshot horsewoman. I chuckle now that I ever thought that. I was as good as some of the amazing horsewomen that I studied side by side with, soaking up whatever I could from the elders I had the good fortune to learn from. I was still a beginner, and I didn't know this.

There's something humbling and freeing to admitting "I don't know" after years of believing I already knew just about everything. I don't. I'm learning. In martial arts, it's called "beginner's mind." Moment after moment, dropping preconceived notions and greeting each experience with curiosity and wonder. *What is this and how is this unfolding?* It's like reconnecting with being a baby, with fresh eyes, no thoughts, no history of this or that to interfere with experiencing the present moment. Reconnecting to who I was when I met Roulette and Penny.

My own healing through therapies and spiritual practices has reopened this connection between the current me and my past baby me. I find myself in this pristine state at times and love it. Mostly, though, I'm on the move, shifting between beginnings and what's next.

CHAPTER 2

Entering the Profession

Ours is not the task of fixing the entire world at once, but of stretching out to mend the part of the world that is within our reach. — CLARISSA PINKOLA ESTES

HELLO, THERAPEUTIC RIDING

IT WAS 1996, decades since I had gone off to boarding school and stopped riding, decades full of travel and personal and professional exploration. I was a clinical social worker recovering from a breast cancer experience—diagnosis, surgeries, and treatments—when a newspaper ad jumped out at me. A local therapeutic riding center was offering to train volunteers. I followed my curiosity. I wanted to learn more. Volunteering there became the entry point for my involvement with the therapeutic riding profession, and reconnected me with this love of horses that had endured through decades of adventures in meditation, body awareness, and therapies to heal the relationship wounds from my childhood. It also led to my owning Kacee, my first horse since Penny.

Learning to be a volunteer included relearning to groom a horse, using muscles I'd forgotten existed. Aching arms and legs exhausted from standing, even for fifteen minutes. It was too much at first. I was stunned by how weak I was and how uncertain I was about all things horsey. I had considered myself a horse person, yet the knowledge from those years of lessons, showing, teaching, owning, and caring for my own horses was gone—tucked away in some far reaches of my memory banks.

My health challenges explained my weakness, but not the shame of being unable to make circles with a curry comb as part of cleaning the horse. My heart was heavy. I didn't say a word to anyone. I paused frequently to rest, letting my arms hang at my sides, resting my head on the horse's shoulder, or stepping away to sit on a bale of hay down the aisle as tears slid down my cheeks. Would I ever feel stronger, last longer? Would I last at all? Would I remember the names of grooming tools, the names of horse body parts, the traditional sequence of grooming? Would my body again feel the instinctual alertness around these precious but still-wild animals? My survival urges were buried under years of seeking to be normal to fit in, subsumed under the layers of a well-socialized, middle-class girl—under the layers of terror and pain from cancer, from surgeries and chemotherapy, from an uncounted number of frightening life experiences that started in infancy. But I persisted, regaining strength and knowledge, and graduated from grooming horses to leading them during lessons.

The program director there was a gifted visionary and therapeutic riding activist. She attracted eager volunteers like me and steered us to our next level of challenge and helpful functioning in her therapeutic riding program. She was the first to plant the seeds of my becoming an instructor. My self-esteem didn't match her confidence in me, not yet. Shame and self-doubt constrained my urges, dulled my passions.

In Service to the Vulnerable Ones

Years later I was ready to combine my passion for horses with my professional background. My business name then was The Horsey Therapist, reflecting my multiple roles: facilitating horses, humans, and humans together with their horses to develop the best relationships possible. I do not think that horses are therapists—they are more like vulnerable clients. They do have a therapeutic influence simply by being in our lives when we are open to experiencing their essential horseness. When we can attune silently with their nature. Nothing more. If a horse is part of a therapy or learning activity with humans, it is their presence that helps us become present—that is how we are benefited. Horses themselves are assisted by us when we humans take our own learning and growth seriously.

An integration of my spiritual, therapeutic, and body awareness interests was emerging. My passion to advocate for beings without verbal language matched my passion for horses. I had burning embers in my belly when I saw misunderstandings and assumptions about the needs of unborn and newborn humans, of humans of any age who live without verbal capacities, and the vast array of non-human animals. I'm certain this is a residual gift from surviving preverbal trauma myself: the disrupted bonding caused by the common practice of sedating the mother (hence infant, too) during childbirth; and then there was the fear of closeness that resulted from when my brother suffocated me.

I learn experientially, nonverbally, through trial and error—a kinesthetic learner. Animals without language, like our horses, learn this way, too. It makes sense that I've wanted to speak up for others in ways that I missed in my youth. Looking back, it wasn't clear that anyone considered my need to feel accepted and like I belonged, even though by external standards I lived comfortably, with privilege.

Similarly, I wanted the horses to be understood, to be seen, to be accepted. They had helped me so much. Horses like Penny who showed up in relationship with me, standing quietly while I expressed a depth of pain and despair that no humans in my life had welcomed or even acknowledged. The horses did not turn away. They did not try to soothe me into silence with logic, with promises, or with cookies. They saved my spirit. They ignited hope for the possibility of connection. To this day, horses show up every time I show up. I owe my life to them. I am indebted forever and ever. This is why I've tried so hard to repay this debt.

I'm far from perfect, yet I feel deep agony when I fail horses and when I witness others failing them. This failure is maintained by our own inability to be present and regulated. We don't have to stay in failure—there's always the possibility to learn from our mistakes and try again. There's always the possibility to get help to become more regulated.

Horses in captivity rely on us for water, food, shelter, and companionship. They prefer to have more choices than most of us can offer them, especially regarding space and companionship. Being present is also on the list of what horses need from us. And not that many of us can do that yet: show up with honesty and vulnerability about our insides, our pains and joys, struggles, shame, our needs. Being present with our horses is a big step.

Pretending—to feel different on the outside than we feel on the inside—doesn't work with horses. They can't make sense of our pretense. I myself struggle to make sense of pretense even though I understand from an intellectual perspective that we all have parts, and some parts protect us from the feelings of woundedness of other parts. Protection with the sole purpose of survival. Protection that involves hiding those memories of overwhelming experiences that live on in our cells, locked off from our current day-to-day life. Protection because we cannot have all our pain in the room at once. We cannot do that and survive. We have to have only a little bit of pain surface at a time, and deal with that little bit.

This is one theme of my woundedness: the trauma of not fitting in, and not receiving the support and direction needed in order to understand how to fit in. This is about me. And if there's any universality of my experience, this is also about our horses.

In college I researched and wrote a paper called, "The Neglect of the Neglected," highlighting how children with broken bones got attention from Child Protective Services but neglected, quiet children slipped through the cracks. They did not get attention or help. The silent ones were ignored, overlooked. The loudly protesting ones or physically hurt ones got attention. I'm not sure much has changed since then.

Horses live in a world of feeling, in a world without our human words. That's where I live more often than not, although I've learned to live in both worlds, awkwardly at times but with success most of the time. Part of me is in the world of words, and part of me is in the world without words.

My work as a therapeutic riding instructor was close to being the perfect job for me, enabling me to bring together my passion for horses and for people without speech. But there was a glitch. As much as therapeutic riding benefited the riders, the instructors, the volunteers, and the community as a whole, I struggled to find how it benefited the horses. Yet they were keystones—and they still are—to the magnificent things that happen for people with differences, disabilities, and neurodivergence. The horse's point of view was missing, and this disturbed me.

Meanwhile, I wonder how I can lend a hand to those who are on a path of honesty about their pain and needs. How can I help those who want a better relationship with themselves and their horses? We all, horses and humans alike, have the same need for safe relationships, for feeling safe, for finding comfort in the company of others. Yet we are so accustomed to pretending, living as if things are okay when really on so many levels they are not.

Time for Changes

Years ago I was drawn to situations where I could facilitate people changing. It started with bodywork, body awareness, and therapeutic massage. It expanded through breath awareness work, rebirthing, and in the early 1990s, I arrived on the doorstep of clinical social work. I shifted from addressing change in the body to addressing change in the mind, developing an integrated approach which reflected my belief that we are body/mind—all one thing, interconnected within ourselves as well as interconnected with all other living beings.

I was well on my way to full-fledged burnout as a mental health clinician in 2011 when I started learning Somatic Experiencing®, a trauma resolution method developed by Peter Levine. The personal sessions required for the training impacted me both personally and professionally, renewing my excitement about working with people, and freeing me from some habitual relationship patterns that had left me feeling small and unworthy. I went on to become a teaching assistant for Somatic Experiencing®, exposing myself again and again to the principles and practices. I often say Somatic Experiencing® also saved my life. It allowed my intrinsic, well-regulated nervous system to emerge from below layers of everyday, medical, and interpersonal traumas—as well as the more commonly recognized traumatic events like car accidents, falling on my head, and breaking bones.

These changes affected my horsemanship, too. I used to rely on direction from those teachers who helped me navigate my relationships with horses. I found teachers who helped me figure out a few things about myself as well. These experiences brought an expanded awareness that has been more valuable than any new technique. I started to think for myself, to trust what I was observing and interpreting about the horse's behaviors and needs, finding my way to what works through trial and error. I'm still finding my way. Each horse's learning needs are unique, and I'm intent on figuring those out. I want to make the learning process as easy as possible. I'm left feeling proud of what I learned and sometimes also ashamed of my mistakes—an interesting combination. Perhaps this book will serve as a collection of directional arrows, helping someone learn by eavesdropping on my process.

My years working as a clinical social worker refined and deepened my understanding of and empathy for people who feel disconnected and full of pain. Personal growth through my own therapy enriched what I learned in school and in professional settings. Therapy helped me release residual relational pain from childhood. I brought all of this to therapeutic riding.

I loved my work as a PATH Intl. Therapeutic Riding Instructor, yet I struggled with the contradiction between our mission to help people with a wide range of disabilities and our habit of mislabeling and dismissing therapy horses who showed signs of distress. Some of the therapy horses had bad reputations due to normal horse behaviors—like biting and kicking—that were scary and unwelcome in lessons. I wondered how much these horses were misunderstood when their behaviors triggered fear responses in humans. I wondered if those responses reinforced the relationship problems rather than resolved them. I knew that we humans sometimes cope with distress by placing blame and viewing situations in a negative light. I wondered if we could instead feel our own discomfort, while also marveling at what is mysterious, confusing, or upsetting, then seek ways to repair and reconnect after an upset.

When therapy horses are labeled problematic because of scary behaviors, it is easy to alleviate the situation by concluding they are burned out and then finding them a new home. If a horse kicks or bites, or is considered lazy or stubborn, we surmise that it doesn't like its job, doesn't belong in the therapy program, and would be happier doing something else. We say goodbye to the horse, relocating it out of our daily awareness, and look for a new, good horse to replace the not-so-good one we moved away. All because we didn't know how to help that horse feel good about its involvement in our program routines.

I wondered if I could facilitate changing the minds of both the horses and the humans (instructors and volunteers), improving their relationships to foster the consistent sense of competence and safety that was missing.

I started asking questions. I figured if I could learn to be with and handle horses in new ways, then others could, too. "So, this horse has a reputation of kicking? When did that start? Does she kick everyone or just some people? What happens before she kicks? And this horse who has a rep for biting—does he bite every time? Does he bite everyone? What happens before he bites?"

All this questioning fueled my drive to offer help to the horses. I wanted to see if my budding theory about preventing burnout was applicable. Our horses display behaviors as a communication to us. If we can offer our listening and support before the unwanted behaviors arise, while keeping our horses physically fit and feeling emotionally safe, could we keep these horses we love so much in our therapy programs? Could we bring about the changes needed so the unwanted behaviors would recede or cease, and be replaced by the behaviors we wanted?

The first time I attended a clinic (a gathering of horsemanship students seeking help) taught by horsemanship clinician, author, musician, and Aikidoist, Mark Rashid, I asked him, "What can I do to help the horses in the therapeutic riding program where I work? Some of them have developed the habit of nipping the volunteers who lead them during lessons, and it disturbs the volunteers and the riders as well."

Mark's answer was simple. "Get different leaders."

I thought about his answer a lot. Although we were not going to dismiss the current program volunteers and seek new ones, we could bring new information to them so they could in fact be different with the horses. That is what I started doing, offering training in horse-handling techniques and in self-awareness to the program staff as well as the volunteers.

Teaching and Differences

It fascinates me how much overlap there is between being a teacher of horses and a teacher of people, whether those people are neurodivergent (with or without disabilities or trauma) or neurotypical. Perhaps there is a continuum of differences based on genetics, brain development, emotional intelligence, physiological states, and ease of access to the frontal lobe and complex thinking brain that has been so valued in our culture.

I do my best to respond with patience, curiosity, determination, creativity, and knowledge in all of my roles: riding instructor, horse trainer, and somatic psychotherapist and educator. When I am in a calm state, I can pause for the momentary opportunities to arise when I can learn more about myself or my students. No two beings are alike at all. The differences I notice and honor help me be a better person, and hence a better teacher.

The success of communication falls to me, not the riding students or the horses. Most therapeutic students will show me their confusion with how they respond to a request. I might say, "Ride to the red cone and stop," and the rider rides to the red cone and stops. No confusion there. With another student, I might say, "Ride to the red cone and stop," and the rider might hear, "Ride to the red pole and stop," then proceed to ride to the red pole and keep walking. Something in the communication system is not working.

I tend to start looking first for what I might change, such as choosing different words, or checking with the student to see how my instruction was understood. Then I wonder about the rider's current state. Are emotions, internal monologues, or physical discomforts interfering with listening, absorbing, or deciding how to act on new input?

Similarly, a horse will not ask me how to be more balanced when we are doing a turn on the hindquarters, but when I notice the horse's distress, I can check my own balance and adjust my request. With horses and humans, first I notice, then I adjust, and then I pay attention to how my suggestions or directions are received.

I learned to set goals within my scope of practice as a therapeutic riding instructor. Although I couldn't focus on a rider's ankle mobility if that rider had cerebral palsy, I could help that rider feel more balanced and more in tune with the horse, despite flexibility limitations.

When a rider had residual fear from a past experience that was affecting her ability to be assertive and clear without emotion—such as a fall off a horse, or an unresolved disruption in a human relationship—I would invite us to talk about the subterranean stuff that was interfering. This wasn't a conversation we would have in the first few lessons, but when I heard riders expressing frustration or anger at themselves or their horses, I responded to that likely subterranean stuff, and not just to their balance, their posture, or their timing. Of course, not all riders were open to these deeper conversations, but the ones who continued to ask for lessons with me had learned—and accepted—that this was part of what I would offer.

This shift also influenced my approach with horses. Rather than impose my agenda, I was learning to adjust my focus to fit what the horse was ready to do that day. I may have wanted a better halt, but it was more important that the horse was feeling okay with what we were doing.

With both horses and humans, I keep getting better at observing, so I can perceive their communications with more accuracy. Both species have the ability to communicate very clearly, regardless of anybody's ability to notice and accurately interpret what is meant.

Entering

When entering a *dojo*, tradition has us pause, bow as an act of respect, and then step left foot first into the room where we will be practicing. This sequence developed in the era when a samurai wore his sword hanging from his belt on the left side, allowing easy access as he reaches with his right hand across his body to grasp the hilt, draw the sword, and prepare for battle. To enter with the left foot first handicaps the one entering. It is physically awkward to step forward with your left foot while reaching across your body to grasp the sword. Stepping with the left foot, therefore, became a statement: *I come unarmed. I come in peace.*

This is how I want to enter any space, whether it is a *dojo*, or a friend's home, or a relationship with another being. *I come unarmed. I come in peace.*

To be unarmed means not only coming without weapons, but also without preconceptions or prejudices. Thoughts and beliefs can cause as much as damage as physical harm does. Paradoxically, thoughts and beliefs can also be the balms that soothe the deepest of wounds.

Kindness and curiosity are two words which bring me to the present moment with openness instead of assumptions. Bringing kindness with my curiosity helps me mold a story of goodness and possibility of goodness. These words are inscribed in my brain and rooted in my heart.

In psychotherapeutic circles, when we practice finding a neutral reason why something happened, empty of blame or attribution of meanness, we call it *benign interpretation*. An example might be that you think, "They didn't respond to me because they just lost their dog, not because they hated me and wanted to exclude me." I learned of benign interpretation from my father. My father learned it in a family therapy program with my older brother. It was an unexpected—and precious—gift for me from them both. It still helps me find my way to pausing when I start to blame or feel sorry for myself, when I start to travel with my thoughts and emotions down a well-worn path that has little resemblance to what's actually happening.

The entrance to life starts at conception, when we are imprinted with patterns we will reenact throughout life. From this, we move forward and take risks because life requires us to keep changing, adapting. We enter relationships and question, "Am I safe here?" We encounter unfamiliar places or social groups, wondering about these transitions: "Where have I been and where am I going?" We enter the world of horses and healing with openness to learn about connecting, despite species differences. We enter the realm of awakening as we recognize the impact of traumas we've experienced, and the impact of traumas our horses have experienced. We enter into learning new ways to relate so that we can heal.

We can enter newness with trust that we will resolve wounds from past experiences and find freedom from prejudices. Isn't it when we become childlike again that the wonders of the world are available to us—wonders like getting along with horses, understanding and responding to their needs? And isn't being childlike the fresh, open state of being, uncluttered by life's baggage?

Entering into this childlike state where trust and play, movement and rest and adventure are all equal parts of daily life: this is my goal, to bring this to all relationships.

Part Two: Survival 101

CHAPTER 3

Safe, Fearful, and Beyond

To be "well" is not to live in a state of perpetual safety and calm, but to move fluidly from a state of adversity, risk, adventure, or excitement, back to safety and calm, and out again. Stress is not bad for you; being stuck is bad for you.
— EMILY NAGOSKI AND AMELIA NAGOSKI

AM I SAFE WITH YOU?

IT WAS RUSTY'S TURN for some quiet time being groomed and saddled in the paddock behind the barn. I didn't halter or tie him. He knew the routine and when he was feeling safe and mentally with me, he needed nothing to keep him close.

Our ride was different that day. I was still figuring out how I could encourage a more open, forward movement on his part. When I asked (and sometimes asked and asked and asked), he would give me forward movement. But that was not what I wanted. I wanted his enthusiasm. I knew it was there inside him. I had some guesses about what I'd done inadvertently to squash it. I had some ideas how to invite it back out.

I wasn't expecting a one-time, life-changing event with him, but that day was good. And I was glad I was riding in my secure-feeling Western saddle. Glad because my ability to hold on to that saddle's horn and cantle gave me confidence to experiment with liberating Rusty from his reservations when I said, "Let's go."

First, I mounted him, asked him to move, and rode him wherever he went, without picking up the reins. Mostly his interest was at the arena gate where he would be closest to his herd mates who were grazing on the other side of the barn. I remembered a friend suggesting I should lead my horse away from where he wanted to be, and then mount and let him carry me to his desired spot. So, I dismounted and led Rusty to the other end of the arena. It was easy to mount from the fence. As I climbed up the wooden rails, he stepped into position near me parallel to the fence and stopped, just as we'd practiced over and over. Once I had mounted, I livened up a little, asking him to start moving by feeling the walking motion in my body, and again he headed off at a walk toward the gate at the other end.

I livened up some more and he broke into a half-hearted trot for the rest of the way. I dismounted and led him to the other end again. I mounted and off we went, this time with a little more life in his trot and a few canter steps, but still I had the sense he was holding back.

The next time I offered more life as we headed off. He took a stride or two and then let go into his own unrestrained liveliness—no holding back. This felt like a leap, a buck, a bigger leap followed by a bigger buck, and a couple of canter strides followed by some large loose trotting before he slowed down.

I was glad I was holding on to the horn and cantle for that ride. I was even gladder that I did nothing mentally or physically to interfere with this offering of liveliness. This was huge progress for me managing my fear reactions. If I had pulled on the reins, he would have experienced the same old discouragement and inhibition and might never want to let himself loosen up with me again.

Again I dismounted, led him to the other end, mounted, and livened up. This time he responded with more of the bigger, looser trot that I'd seldom felt from him. That response confirmed that he could do it, and more importantly, that I was able to get out of his way, allowing him the freedom to move like that.

After this, I played around with offering a little life—enough to discourage him from stopping—as we got close to the gate, his destination, and then observing where he took me. We did quite a few small circles right near the gate before he left this pattern and headed off toward the middle of the arena. In that moment, as in many others, he seemed very keen on listening to me and getting it right. I liked that he could be obedient, but I didn't want it to stop there. I wanted him to try things without fear of my criticizing him.

After I dismounted, I decided to see if he would go to the barn with me without my handling his halter and lead rope, so I draped the end of the lead rope over his back. I went to the gate and he followed me. I opened the gate and let him through and then turned to close the gate, unsure whether he'd stay near me or head off on his own. He kept walking until he got to some bare ground where he sniffed around while I approached him, passed him, and headed to the barn. Seeing that he hadn't come with me, I took a few steps back to him and lightly touched his lead rope, then turned for the barn again. This time he followed. It felt good. I was feeling our connection and trusting that staying connected was important to him as well as to me. This mammalian need to feel safe and connected was something we shared.

All of this required me to be in the present moment with him. Me wandering around in some mental fantasy of some other time and place—yesterday or tomorrow—severs our connection. This has long been my imperfect meditation practice, being present with myself and with others.

I found myself thinking about Rusty and his confusion, which seemed to be very much like my confusion. I may have been projecting this on him, but I enjoyed my musings about parallels and similarities.

I think Rusty confused direction with criticism. I take all blame for the many times I said to him, "No, not that!" How many times does it take for a horse to hear "No!" before he feels discouraged? When I went to direct him, he was expecting to be criticized. I could tell that did not feel good to him. His expectation brought with it a mental brace, an emotional cringing, and physical reluctance. It was my responsibility to monitor myself, to let him have whatever new experiences he needed of moving and being around me and carrying me places, thus building a new, more pleasant memory bank of time with me.

I had faith we could both make some changes. I suspected it would be easier for him to let go of expecting criticism from me than it would be for me to let go of expecting criticism from people in my life. In fact, I still do misinterpret simple observations as criticism.

A few days later, I was ready for another ride with Rusty. I had procrastinated through the day so that it was getting cold and dark by the time I saddled up and led him to the arena. Normally I would not have saddled him up, thinking it wasn't a good time to ride. I was willing to take this risk in hopes of more opportunities for me to feel safe with Rusty.

Rusty offered me more energy and willingness to tool around that day than I could have imagined. What a treat, this good feeling! That was what it felt like to have a horse carry you someplace. His reluctance was gone. His cranky ears were gone. His choppy trot was gone. The "make me" feeling was gone. I was amazed how quickly things had changed from the old impasse, that conflict between the urge to fight and the urge to flee. He trotted out at length. He cantered around easily, making the transition in response to a light request from me. He took me places at the walk, the trot, the canter. He asked about slowing and stopping and sometimes I said yes and sometimes I said, "Let's go further."

My heart was overflowing with appreciation for these riding moments with Rusty. I was speechless with thanks for my life circumstances which allowed me the time to spend with the animals. Friends and professionals guided me as I learned how to train Rusty and how to get along with him. Although I had introduced Rusty to saddles, bridles, and carrying a rider, most of our riding at that point had been in horsemanship clinics, with a few short rides outside the clinic arenas with other horses and riders.

It remained a mystery how practicing riding skills and communicating better with Rusty in an arena, might translate to some trail riding adventures. I had an abundance of tolerance for Rusty's lively expressions, but I was unsure if my riding buddies and their horses would also tolerate them. I was unsure how well I could teach Rusty the contradictory ideas that his enthusiastic outbursts were welcome play in the arena, but those same enthusiastic outbursts were not welcome on trail rides. I was in no hurry to test out Rusty's understanding of the tension between those two ideas and risk upsetting or causing injury to my riding buddies, whose safety and comfort zones I needed to consider. I wanted them to feel safe enough to include me in group trail rides. *Please don't leave me out.*

I wondered what conditions I would want for testing out a trail ride alone with Rusty. Would I do what I'd been doing in the arena: lead him away from where he wants to be, mount, invite him to move, hold on to horn and cantle, and see where—and how fast— he wanted to take me? I suspected I would deal with that after a few more rides in the confinement of the arena, where I had made it clear that his liveliness was welcome. There I could start experimenting with nurturing his enthusiasm as I directed him. I attempted that when I felt our togetherness. I rotated open my left leg to invite him to head to the left, which he did. This was my way of having fun and engaging with Rusty when we both felt safe. It felt like dancing with a familiar partner, with a large empty dance floor to enjoy.

Pause Button

Benji was possibly the most popular, most ridden therapy horse I had ever met. A big and balanced middle-aged Belgian draft horse, he brought his training, experience, and calm demeanor to riders of all sizes, ages, and abilities.

Benji was like a lot of draft horses, and his tendency to be slow to react and have a long pause button helped mollify the worries of his riders.

A pause button is one of our best tools in all aspects of life. It allows us to interrupt a reaction, think about what's happening, and choose the best action. Physiologically, it allows us to regain access to our neocortex, which houses the executive thinking parts of our brain. Regaining that access is especially important after something has triggered a threat response.

We have automatic survival instincts running the show all the time. We notice a potential danger or threat, like a crack of thunder or a car backfiring, or a small movement like a mouse scurrying across the floor, or a tone of voice that is louder and higher-pitched or lower-pitched than usual, such as a shriek or a bellow. We are startled.

We are wired to orient to what startled us, looking to know, "Are you friend or foe?" If it might be foe, then we ready ourselves for flight if we can or fight if we can't flee to safety. When our subconscious deems neither of those strategies optimal for our survival, then we become immobilized in the freeze or collapse responses. (Some discussions of survival strategies now identify another autonomic coping strategy, fawning—often described as pleasing or appeasing behaviors—but in this book I will focus on the more widely known: find/engage, flight, fight, freeze, and collapse.)

Our brains make all of these determinations subconsciously and super quickly, and often based on the past success of certain survival strategies. If previously I survived by collapsing, then my collapse response will be the first to show up under threat. Likewise, if I survived by fighting, my first survival instinct to show up will be to fight. Humans and horses share these hardwired, deep instincts—and some but not all of us have developed an ability to pause and make choices rather than letting our instincts run the show.

Therapeutic riding instructors like me value horses who can pause before running off. And the longer the pause, the better. Some horses run first, and stop to ask questions after they've used up their rush of flight chemicals. Other horses pause for a millisecond, scanning for an indication whether it's safe to resume grazing or it's time to run for their lives. When we aren't communicating the equine version of *Relax, we're safe*, that horse will be running before we register its mini-pause. A horse like Benji, with a long pause button, is especially fantastic and worth every penny spent on upkeep. This horse will stop and wait, relatively unbothered by whatever surprising sound or sight. The safety of the whole teaching team is almost guaranteed when a therapy horse has a long pause button. We can count on this horse to act as if nothing scary has happened, safely carrying an unstable or timid rider. Rusty, for example, would not make a good therapy horse because if something were to surprise him, he would stop, stiffen, and then bolt with no concern other than staying alive.

I've seen a few therapeutic riding lessons go awry when the horse got scared. The sidewalkers—the volunteers who walk along in a lesson close enough to rest their hands or arms on the horse's back as they support the rider—had their own fear responses kick in when the horse's did. I know from experience the uncontrollable urge to move away from a scared horse turning ninety degrees or running a few steps with no warning. These volunteers later shared they felt ashamed and disappointed with themselves because they didn't stay in position. Even though we humans can't move as fast as the horses, the volunteers blamed themselves because the rider's safety had been compromised, and they feared my scorn or disappointment. Their sense of being a welcome and trustworthy part of the teaching team was shaken. I wanted nothing more than for them to know that our survival responses happen instantly—before we notice—before we can stop our instinctive action. This is especially true when stress is high and we ourselves can't access our pause buttons.

Benji's pause button worked when our pause buttons failed, when the impulse to protect ourselves overrode our intention to stay close to the rider during a lesson. Benji wasn't bothered by changes in the environment, nor by the moods and behaviors of his riders, nor by the casual approach of instructor and volunteers—casual, because we counted on his pause button.

Safe, Fearful, and Beyond: Autonomic Nervous System Basics

To better understand how both horses and humans react to perceived threats—and how to work with those reactions—it helps to have a basic understanding of the autonomic nervous system, which governs those instinctive responses. This is familiar to me now, but I remember my eyes glazing over when I first heard the words "sympathetic" and "parasympathetic." I hope to keep things simple enough that you won't do what I did: run to the fridge for some comfort food or head off to check email—anything to turn my attention away from what threatens to be overwhelming.

We mammals survive because we can detect safety, danger, and life threats, and because we can take action, either mobilizing to connect with safe others (find) or to fight or flee from threats and danger. We also survive by freezing or collapsing, two states of immobilization.

We are hardwired for survival. The autonomic nervous system is automatic, working day and night whether we pay attention to it or not, and whether we like it or not. Who chooses to blush or break out into a nervous sweat? Who wants to lose bladder control when terrified? Who wants to sit silently watching something horrific happen nearby? What horse enjoys running away from herd, food, and shelter when something scary happens?

Even though I know in my mind that Rusty would never intentionally hurt or threaten me, I am easily scared by him. I have fallen off more than once after he startled and moved abruptly, and he has kicked me, leaving a big bruise on my left thigh when I unwittingly walked between him and the horse he was aiming for. I may always flinch first when his movement surprises me, then breathe a sigh of relief when his action doesn't end with my being injured.

Traditionally, the autonomic nervous system has two branches: the sympathetic nervous system and the parasympathetic nervous system. These two systems are often described using the analogy of the gas pedal and brakes.

The sympathetic nervous system is like the gas pedal. In moderation, it gets us going for day-to-day activities like getting up in the morning, taking a shower, or cooking a meal. Fully engaged—pedal to the metal—it fuels us to respond to danger through our flight and fight responses.

The parasympathetic nervous system is like the brake system. These brakes, when applied in moderation, slow us down, allowing for resting and digesting, and for quiet times of meditating, communing with nature, or feeling safe being engaged with and physically close to someone. In extreme moments of threat, these same brakes bring us to a full stop via the collapse response.

There is also the full stop of the freeze response, a mix of sympathetic and parasympathetic states.

All of our autonomic nervous system experiences are blends of sympathetic and parasympathetic states. I can be having tea with a friend (moderate sympathetic and moderate parasympathetic with safe engagement), then my mind drifts to an upcoming dental procedure (higher sympathetic and disconnect from the parasympathetic social contact state). We might notice ourselves shifting in infinite variations along the continuum from *I'm safe* to *I'm in danger* to *my life is threatened.*

The autonomic nervous system works in cycles—of activation, discharge, settling, integration, and completion—when it can, when it's not stuck. My memories of sitting near the ocean on the coast of Maine make it easy for me to think of these cycles as waves. Waves build, they reach their crest and break, and settle. Then there's a pause before the next wave builds.

Often these cycles—especially in the settling phase—are interrupted by emergency circumstances or even by the misplaced kindness of others. Think of how discombobulating it is to tumble off a horse and plummet to the ground. The sympathetic activation increased as soon as we started to lose our balance. It continued as we gripped with anything we could—hoping to prevent the fall—and then tried to minimize injury using our hands and arms to protect our faces and brains.

When the quiet place for allowing the sympathetic activation to discharge isn't available or is discouraged—*You're fine, let's get you up and back on that horse*—then the natural discharge process is thwarted, the incomplete protective reactions remain unexpressed, and the released biochemicals remain locked in our bodies. Well-intentioned onlookers want to encourage us to get up and carry on. Perhaps it will soothe them to see proof that their family member or friend is unharmed. But for those waves to complete after a fall, or another highly activating event, we should first rest in the company of someone safe, allowing the discharge (shaking, sweating, or tears for example) to happen and the settling to begin. (By the way, this can happen years later.)

My studies of attachment and bonding have helped me appreciate feeling safe with someone as our primary survival strategy. Think about the infant in the arms of a safe parent or caregiver. Soft eye contact, touch, breathing together, smiling—these are aspects of a calm parasympathetic state and our attachment system in action. We all are wired to experience this sense of safety and connection. Sadly, many of us have early relational wounds that left us chronically feeling unsafe in relationships. Unintentional, and often secondary to early medical interventions, these wounds have limited the capacity to trust and feel at ease with another human being. How many of us feel safer with horses or dogs or other animals than with people?

Horses can have attachment wounds as well. And as Rusty's owner, I've found ways to support our connection in order to help him, more so since I started doing my own attachment healing. When I am in the calm of a parasympathetic state, I can help him settle and connect. Benji, on the other hand, needed less regulation from humans than Rusty does.

CHAPTER 4

Feeling Safe

Devote yourself to your partner's sense of safety and security and not simply to your idea about what that should be. What may make you feel safe and secure may not be what your partner requires from you. Your job is to know what matters to your partner and how to make him or her feel safe and secure. — STAN TATKIN

ENERGIZED AND CONNECTED

I DIDN'T USUALLY spend all day with the horses, but that Tuesday I did. I had the day off from work and decided to immerse myself in learning. I had brought Kacee, Rusty, and Prince to the arena and let them loose. They were lively, kicking up their heels at each other, running off, and coming back for more. I stood at the gate and watched, feeling my heart beat a bit stronger each time the bunch of them headed in my direction. They quieted after a few minutes and started nibbling at bits of grass along the fence line. I quieted too, and started thinking about what to do next.

I chose Prince first, the big copper bay Arab gelding. I knew he hated having the deworming paste plunged into his mouth from a plastic tube—a common healthcare practice to reduce a horse's worm load—so I'd brought along an empty tube, figuring I might start to help him feel better about this. I wasn't surprised that he pulled his head away when I touched the tube to his lips. I waited until he let me draw his head close again. My goal was for him to calmly accept this procedure, although if I could have forced him to stand still, I would have. A part of me wanted him to change right then and there.

I remained as focused and calm as I could be, wanting to avoid adding more emotional disturbance to Prince's already worried state. While intent on completing what I'd started, I began to understand why horsemanship clinicians joke about packing a lunch before they commence working with some horses. I was doing this on horse time, relinquishing my human clock and determining "time's up" based on the horse's time frame. I waited for Prince to make some changes, not for the clock to announce that we were done.

It took about ten minutes before Prince allowed me to touch the corner of his mouth with the tube without pulling away. I sighed and thanked him. Waiting for a horse to offer some small sign of readiness was progress for me, and I was pleased, and mindful enough not to ask for more.

I turned to Kacee, who was standing nearby, and invited her to walk with me across the arena without halter or lead rope. I kept an eye on Rusty because he was eyeing us. I feared he might come join us in a rambunctious way, and that thought made my stomach tight. *I might get hurt.* But he didn't; he stood and watched.

After Kacee and I walked around together, I decided for my Rusty time I would take him away from the other horses and back to the barn. My initial thought was to do something to help bring his energy to a calmer state before haltering him—like ask him to trot or canter—because I expected him to get upset when I took him away from the others. But Rusty approached me and wouldn't leave. Although he was in a lively mood, he did not barge into my space. I changed my mind about him moving out to expend some energy, deciding to see how much trust I could offer him, to be close and not do anything that would trigger my fear.

I walked off down the arena and Rusty came along—head high, neck arched, nostrils wide, energized and ready for who-knows-what. I took a breath in and exhaled to calm myself before jogging off toward the cavalettis (a series of poles on the ground). He jogged right along with me, nice as could be. I slowed and stopped. He slowed and stopped. I reversed direction and he swung around. We headed off again over the cavalettis. Back down over them again and returned again. I realized even with his energy as lively as it was, he was mentally with me. I held out the halter and he put his nose into the noseband, standing still even though he was revved up. I attached the lead rope and we walked off together to the gate and out, down the slope to the barn. He was fully mannered and self-contained, and so was I. I did not bug him to slow or back off or anything. I allowed him to be this spirited and trusted him to be listening and not bump into me.

I started to think about riding him when his energy was like that. I usually employed all the nifty things I'd learned about how to calm a horse, and now I could explore how to direct this aliveness instead of shutting him down. Staying connected during groundwork (the unmounted activities) was success. My fear did not interfere. The next steps would be to continue to help him believe all that friskiness would be welcome when I was riding him, and help me have faith I could direct it, so that both of us could enjoy our time together.

I had stretched my limits some and felt okay about what had transpired. I was starting to feel safe with Rusty when he wasn't in a more subdued mood. For the most part, I remained emotionally neutral through what I liked to call learning opportunities. I did freeze a bit, but I could witness what I felt and did when scared. I tightened up and held my breath. My awareness of these briefer moments of reactivity was new. And then I easily settled back after a little spike of adrenaline.

Can We Give Up the Fight?

I was overcome with sorrow. Peggy had phoned me to complain about Nelson, her newly-purchased two-year-old palomino Quarter Horse. She was sore from wrestling, in her determination to halter him and lead him to her round pen, the 60-foot diameter circular enclosure where she could free lunge him (directing him to move in a circle around her without halter or lead rope) and either teach him or learn from him, I wasn't sure yet.

I've been there and done that, battling with some of my horses earlier in my adult horse-ownership days. There I sat on the other end of the phone call, wondering how to help her engage Nelson's sense of curiosity about what she was asking—an approach that had helped me with my horses. If Nelson could start to understand rather than defend himself, he could figure out how to go along with her ideas. I knew it was possible for Peggy to have an easier experience. And I wanted to help Peggy and Nelson feel safe together.

I have a slogan printed on my business cards: *It's our nature to get along.* This goes for horses and for people. Horses are hardwired to get along with other herd animals. If they are fighting us, it is because they perceive us as a threat or they anticipate something unpleasant or painful. It won't ever be safe or fun that way, for us or for the horses. There is no safe and sane way to force a horse to do something.

Horses weigh more than we do, and their awareness of what is happening around them is eons beyond what we are capable of. They spend 24/7 keeping track of their environment. We spend most of our time racing after—and believing—our thoughts, regardless of what our senses are telling us. Horses have a huge advantage over us unless we learn to use our brains to engage their brains, and our nervous systems to calm theirs. Our neocortical brains have a bigger capacity, but that doesn't mean we are using more brain space than they are—or using it more effectively. I have seen little evidence that we humans use brainpower better than horses do, regarding awareness of what is happening moment to moment in the environment.

I was feeling sad and worried. Peggy was approaching Nelson thinking that it was normal to fight to halter him. This approach bothered me—and reminded me of my own scuffles.

I hope that each of us, myself included, will develop the habit of questioning any beliefs that support domination and force.

I hope that each of us will notice when we feel upset and/or threatened by a horse, and should we find ourselves responding with the faulty notion that manhandling the horse will fix things, we will instead seek help to better get along with our horses. Help is available. Help from someone with more horse-handling experience, who understands how to work with a horse's nature, and can simultaneously support us humans.

Horses are wonderful, willing animals, unless we show them that life around humans doesn't offer anything sensible or enjoyable for them—that humans are scary, not safe.

I hope that each of us will challenge our old ways of thinking. We can be amazed again and again—even brought to tears—as we experience how a horse responds when given a choice and when given something to be interested in. What if we each were to explore changing how we approach our horses, and played around with getting things done without force—even without any tack at all—until a better understanding develops between us humans and our equine companions?

He Knows His Job

Amigo was an easygoing, middle-aged horse, highly valued for his help during lessons at a therapeutic riding program where I was an instructor. His movement was soft, and his structure was large and sturdy. He tolerated—at times maybe admitted to enjoying—the attention of people. He was pretty unflappable, hardly blinking an eye when a rider suddenly shrieked or jerked. He wasn't even bothered by the sidewalkers.

He had some behaviors that were not so endearing, however, like pinning his ears and snapping his teeth as he swung his head toward the volunteer leading him. He eventually took a sleeve or two in his mouth and staff started wondering about retiring him, concluding he was burned out, unhappy with his job. He had earned a reputation as a grouchy old man. A grouchy old man who posed a threat to our lesson team. Volunteers and staff weren't feeling safe with him.

Sorrow entered the riding ring, joining admiration and fear. I had so many mixed feelings about this horse. He was patient. He was big. He was steady. He was gentle with the riders. He was scary. My desire to see if I could figure out what he was trying to tell us grew bigger than my hesitation to speak up. I was the newest employee there. Did I know enough to help? Would anyone let me try? Would I fail and feel humiliated? If I succeeded, would anyone recognize my skills and efforts? My fear of being criticized or rejected threatened to undermine my urge to help.

Retirement was a possibility for Amigo, and an honorable one. A therapy horse as healthy and well-trained as he was would move to a home where he would be loved by someone, ridden, and live as nature intended, in the company of other horses. Gone would be the expectation to perform as a team member in the unique atmosphere of a therapeutic riding lesson.

We expect some strange things of our lesson horses. Asking a horse to stand still when fear arises opposes their instinct to run from what's scary. Horses move to find safety and to release the biochemical charge that accompanies being startled. Amigo was loved for his consistent response of "I'm okay with this," even standing still when he was feeling worried. So why the pinned ears and bared teeth?

Despite the talking horse Mr. Ed on TV, we know that horses do not speak as we do. They express their needs and moods with their nonverbal body language. Most of us have been told that ears forward depict a happy horse; ears back can mean an unhappy horse; and ears pressed back against the neck? Watch out, angry horse! Ears sideways can be a sign of pain or boredom. Ears in motion—front, back, and sideways—portray a horse who is alert and curious about what's going on.

In the lesson ring, a horse might shift his attention between the rider, the leader, the instructor, the car that just pulled into the driveway, the parent standing along the wooden fence watching the lesson, and the three horses grazing in a field over yonder. Ears moving, attention shifting, showing interest in his environment—but not alarm—the therapy horse keeps track of all of this and is able to stand still, walk, trot, turn, and stop when requested by his rider or leader.

It was time for me to get to know Amigo. I assumed his behaviors were his way of letting us know that something wasn't okay. I wanted to find out more about his thinking, his likes and dislikes, what he knew and what he might be confused about. I started spending time with him in his paddock when neither of us felt the pressures of a lesson day. I stood near him with no agenda, breathing and softly letting my gaze fall where it wanted. Then, with his consent, I approached and explored touching him all over. I asked him to take one step back, one step forward, to lower his head, to let me hold each foot up off the ground. He was a delight, ready to do most of what I asked. He quickly taught me that he needed very little input from me to do what he knew. His only glitch? He did not show much understanding, willingness, or ability to step backwards. From this casual assessment, I generalized this: Amigo knows the lesson routine and prefers doing his job without anyone micromanaging the whens and hows and wheres. He doesn't need to be told what to do.

I don't like to be told how to do something I already know how to do. I especially don't like when someone takes me by the arm and moves me to where I am already going. I grit my teeth, bracing against the unnecessary instruction. In a resentful huff, I have thoughts like, "This is offensive, belittling, totally uncalled for!" If I were a horse, my ears would be pinned, my tail would be swishing with annoyance, and at some point, I would bite or kick to get my message across: "Let me do my job! I know how to do this. Stop treating me like I don't know what I'm doing!" This was my best interpretation of what Amigo had been trying to communicate to us.

I shared these thoughts with the horse herd coordinator and the team of instructors. I asked them if they'd be willing to experiment with treating Amigo like a kind old uncle who knew quite a few things and was comfortable repeating those things day in and day out. I hoped we would find a way to honor and support his competence and contentment with the lesson routines.

Most horses like routine balanced with novelty. A little novelty—not so much that it's overwhelming their ability to integrate new learning, but not so much routine that it's: ho-hum, bored, bored, bored. Amigo was comfortable being bored, but not content to be micromanaged.

To enable this change in how we thought and acted called for additional education and support for our volunteers and instructors. Some were initially skeptical that horses could know how to do things on their own, that horses had personal preferences about how they were asked to do their job. I designed and proposed some trainings. They were accepted, and I delighted in facilitating them. This was aligned with my personal passion to help the horses and others who cannot speak for themselves.

As Amigo was recognized for his lesson expertise and started to be handled differently, the volunteers resumed feeling safe when leading him, and all of us learned a few things about problem solving with a horse. Each horse is different. Building on what we had learned about Amigo, I wondered about bringing questions to every horse there: "How much direction do you want from me? What will help you feel good about doing your job? What do you need from me? What can I do to support you?"

In these trainings, we focused on leading from further away from Amigo's head, giving him more space, and giving him more subtle cues when we wanted to signal changes of speed or direction. Each participant experienced how a horse can follow our direction and speed without our pulling or even taking the slack out of the lead rope. These trainings also intended to help the volunteers become more aware of the subtle signs of Amigo's moods. A twitch of the nostrils, a change in his breathing pattern, stiffness through his head and neck, eyes squinting, ears more frequently back—all of these observations came with the goal of noticing his earliest signs of moving from calm and contented to grumpy and irritable.

The sooner we could respond to a horse's body language, the less we would have to do to help him feel better. So instead of having to remove Amigo from the lesson program and his familiar herd environment, we became consciously grateful for his easygoing, knowledgeable job performances. We apologized for our human errors, our failures to notice his requests for space and independence. We started working in harmony with him, meeting his needs to feel safe with us. We watched him blossom in his role as a sought-after therapy horse.

Newness Again and Again

As the volunteers were learning new ways to handle Amigo, Mike was learning how to ride. He was full of smiles and questions and uncertainty. In fact, due to dementia, he was trying something new each week.

"Oh, I'm going to ride a horse? I've never done that before. I'd like to try it."

His son had signed him up for therapeutic riding lessons, wanting more exercise and social contact for his seventy-seven-year-old father.

Mike was cheerful about learning the basic riding skills of holding the reins and using voice commands like "Walk on" and "Whoa." Mostly he liked to reach over and pat the sidewalkers on the head. Thankfully, they were comfortable with his affectionate nature despite this unusual behavior from an adult rider.

He also liked to sing *Moon River* and we joined in with whatever words we knew ... a little equine-assisted choral group.

It wasn't too rare to work with adults, although most of our riders were children, but it was rare to teach people with dementia. Mike's pleasant way of interacting with the team meant our lesson challenges were focused on his balance and strength rather than on his mood or disorientation to time.

I was intrigued by Mike's increasing ability to do what was needed for riding, even though his mind didn't recognize any progress whatsoever. We introduced and reviewed the same skills each week: greeting the volunteers and his horse Amigo; walking to the mounting ramp; mounting with assistance; and riding Amigo at a walk and through turns and stopping. Each transition and each change of direction required various body systems to be responsive and cooperative, adjusting to the changes and keeping Mike upright on a horse. As Mike's instructor, I learned that the body can learn things even when the mind no longer records these new things. He performed better each week despite his inability to recall his recent history of lessons. His memories of what had happened last week were lost, but his body memories were alive and well. Plus, he lived in a state of feeling safe with social contact. This made it easy for his body to be relaxed and adjusting to the activity of horseback riding.

Feeling Safe

Feeling safe is the basis of progress with horses and with people. Mike was eager to ride, even though he didn't remember that he'd ridden the week before. Similarly, he enjoyed the company and support of the teaching team, even though he didn't remember having met any of us before. Amigo brought his own horse sense of confidence to lessons, where changes in the environment that might bother another horse didn't disturb his baseline feelings of trust.

Trust and feeling safe go hand in hand, and that can include literally going hand in hand. Think of the therapeutic riding student who, needing support to walk to the mounting ramp, reaches out to hold the volunteer's or instructor's hand. This student has had good outcomes when relying on others, so trust comes easily when a hand is needed.

Sometimes we trust and we don't even know that's what we're doing. We allow others to direct us, to position our hands or legs, to put us in novel situations without any foreknowledge of what's coming. As a teacher, I couldn't rely on verbally predicting what would happen next for riders with significant cognitive challenges. Again and again, I adjusted how I presented the next step in order to engage the rider's willingness to try. Those who were scared of most everything needed more support to try new things, and needed to spend more time doing what was familiar. Those with confidence would go more easily into the unknown. It's our responsibility as teachers to ensure as much safety as possible, and to avoid overwhelming any nervous system with too much newness at once. This is true for riding students, and this is true for the horses in our care.

There's magic about feeling safe, and it is contagious. The presence of one person feeling safe—physiologically in a socially-connected parasympathetic state—provides the nervous systems of others with the opportunity to start feeling safe. This resonant connectivity can involve touch but doesn't need to. It happens with or without touch, and supports an experience of whole-body connectedness when we no longer need to protect ourselves physically or emotionally.

As a clinical social worker, I was trained to never touch a client. Initially, this suited me because I was awkward about touch. I was raised in a family where distance and coolness accompanied the lack of physical and verbal expressions of affection. I also craved touch, which had led me to learn massage and other hands-on modalities. By the time I began my work as a therapeutic riding instructor, where physical contact is integral for helping many students ride safely, my comfort with touch exceeded my conflict about it.

In a therapeutic riding lesson, instructors and volunteers will touch riders as part of the lesson plan. Some riders need help getting their right leg over the back of the horse as they are mounting. Some riders need sidewalkers alongside their horses, close enough to gently support the riders to keep them balanced on the horse using hands on ankles or lower legs, or simply to offer a tangible sense that someone is there, available. Some riders are afraid they will fall off even when their balance and strength are adequate to keep them on the horse. Some riders need the prompt of a touch on a hand to know that this is their right hand and they will use it to hold the right rein and steer the horse to the right. Touch is also invaluable for helping riders with proprioception: knowing where their bodies are in space.

We touch riders in an emergency dismount, when instructors and volunteers work together to bring riders off and away from their horses as quickly as possible. The emergency may be something that frightens the horse, so literally moving riders away from horses is a way to provide safety when they can't dismount quickly on their own. We take care of safety first and offer an apology later for touching without prior consent.

Even with the youngest riders, we are mindful about touching them, ideally stating why we want to touch them and asking permission each time. "I'd like to offer you some support by placing my hand gently over your ankle. This might help you feel your foot in a position that will help you stay balanced in the saddle. Is it okay for me to touch you?"

It's easy to assume that children welcome touch—that they consent to touch. But that's not necessarily how it is. We have the responsibility with all new students to find out if touch is upsetting, whether due to family discipline styles, violence, medical interventions, sensory preferences, or the need to say no and express agency over their bodies.

Patience is required when a rider is slow to process incoming information. Impatience adds distress, and distress makes it harder to learn, harder to feel safe when riding a horse. As instructors, we do our best to interpret the body language of riders who are nonverbal and whose responses may not be as clear as a head nodding consent or shaking no.

Riders of any age may have the habit of lying about what's okay when responding to authorities, including parents and instructors. They can be uncertain about if and when they are allowed to say no. They may be ambivalent about touch, as I was. Their desire to please those of us in authority may lead them to override the inclination to say no.

When we make contact without advance notice, as in an emergency, how well this is received can depend on our approach and whether we intentionally sense the contact before we actually touch. This is something I learned, and still practice: to connect energetically before touching. It makes a difference to both people and horses.

When a rider is initiating the touch, we do our best to respond graciously to each situation. The gentle touch of a frail elderly rider who reaches out for contact is quite easy to accept. The come-into-your-space go-for-a-hug-without-asking touch of a brawny sixteen-year-old rider may trigger worry instead of warmth.

When needed in therapeutic riding, we explicitly address the social expectations around touch with riders and family members so we can support their particular family customs. This means having a conversation with the parent or caregiver of the rider to learn what is expected by the family, then exploring whether we need to specify a policy about touch in our lesson, and how we would reinforce a pre-existing family practice about touch. We like the ask-first approach to hugs and handshakes, although we often give a high five without verbal permission. Touch at the periphery (hands and feet) of our bodies is usually easier to accept than closer to our core.

When I was actively working as a PATH Intl. riding instructor, I wanted our volunteers to be comfortable letting me know whether they were okay with giving or receiving touch during a lesson. When I sensed volunteers were ready to override their actual likes and dislikes in order to serve the riders—saying yes to touch when inside they wanted to say no—I initiated conversations to check out if touch really was okay in that lesson. I hoped to support the volunteers' needs for boundaries. And I myself needed to accept their choices, despite my interpretation of their body language—as when words say "yes, okay" and body says "nope." I also had to accept how their unspoken obligation to say yes aligned with their self-image as a valuable volunteer.

We asked the students to touch the horses for grooming, for self-regulation, for feeling connected and grateful. But touching the horses came with different rules. We didn't regularly employ the same careful communications and explicit negotiations that we brought to our riders. I would hesitate when I wanted to support the horse's point of view on being touched. I wondered: Whose touch does this horse welcome? Where does this horse like to be touched? What speed and pressure would this horse like today? How could I tell if what we're doing is okay with this horse? How could I educate others about how a horse communicates its needs and preferences? How could I advocate without offending other instructors or volunteers whose prior horse experience was extensive? How could I speak for the horse without disrupting the student's direct relationship with that horse? My conflicted roles and priorities about horses and touch often left me in a state of partial freeze or collapse.

Usually, the horse's face is the first place a person wants to touch. Most of us can read a human face and determine if coming close and touching is welcome. Human faces give us cues of safety and welcome like soft eyes, dilated pupils, relaxed jaws, even a sense of leaning toward the approach. Although a horse's face offers us the possibility of feeling a soft fuzzy muzzle, the horse may not have a genuine yes response to our touch, which makes it a nonconsensual relationship at that point. What a conflict! Riders and volunteers alike (and me, too) so enjoy the feel of a soft muzzle. And not so many of us can read a horse's face for signs of welcomeness. The horses—like the riders, volunteers, and staff—will not feel safe if they cannot determine if, when, and how they are touched.

How do we come to terms with asking a rider to stroke a horse's neck when the rider needs help calming? Or when a volunteer touches a horse for self-soothing? What are the costs and benefits of that? Closeness with a horse is wonderful for many reasons. It can benefit us and it can benefit the horse. But we cannot take the horse's consent for granted. Can we get good at reading body language? Can we notice how our approach impacts the horse, and adjust our plans to accommodate the nonverbal voice of the horse?

Promoting feeling safe becomes a way of life when we are drawn to better serve our horses by changing how we think and act. Our interpretations improve as we become more aware of what our horses express, and their underlying needs. Although these are not formal techniques, we can do things like allowing the horse choices, and refrain from doing things like touching the face without permission. Our changes support connectedness and contentedness in our equine relationships.

We recognize a well human as someone who is impassioned, excited, and enthralled—someone who wakes up each morning yearning to pursue a dream. We recognize a well horse as alert, curious, ready to engage, and eager about what might come next.

CHAPTER 5

When I'm Scared

Trauma compromises our ability to engage with others by replacing patterns of connection with patterns of protection. — DEB DANA

FEAR TAKES OVER

DESPITE THE AWARENESS I've purposely cultivated over the past five decades, I can act counter to my best intentions, often because of fear. Like barking a four-letter swear word that starts with "s" when my mare, Kacee, scooted.

We were traveling alongside a busy roadway, which went under a highway. The sounds of the traffic overhead echoed as cars rushed by us. Kacee got scared and started to move away from what was scary, as quickly as possible.

What did my yelling do to Kacee? She was worried enough to try to flee, and her closest buddy—me on her back—was worried enough to cry out while my body clenched and froze in a determined-to-hold-on posture. This was not how I would have liked to respond, although for ninety percent of our ride, I had felt good about what I offered her for support and direction. Does a horse balance the percentages? Is a horse capable of figuring out, "Oh, that's her again. She freezes when I do, then she relaxes. I won't take her reaction so seriously next time."

I suspect not. Rather, Kacee was worried, and then I added to her worries. So why would she turn to me for help when she was worried? I wasn't there for her—I was consumed by my own fear and survival reactions. My best self was gone. Kacee was scared and abandoned, without the support of someone calm to help her stay calm.

I'm glad I don't get afraid like that every time I ride. I'm glad my horses let me get on them anyway. I know they remember what it's like with me on their back. I like to think they have a cumulative memory. I like to think that if I offer support for a few days, they know I'm okay, and they can feel safe with me. Then I have a fearful, constricted moment, and that lowers their opinion of my company. Then I have several hours of relaxed, go-with-the-flow-while-I-direct-the-flow type of riding, and that raises their opinion of my company. So, at any time, I'm either improving or degrading their opinion of me, based on their overall multitude of experiences with me.

However, I have to think about this some more. I'm not at all certain it's true.

Meanwhile, lesson learned. Don't disregard fear—it has important messages that can help me recognize whether I'm perceiving safety or danger. I want to listen to my fear, because when it accumulates and is carried from the past, it clouds today's possibilities.

Bronc Ride Breakthroughs

Rusty was anxious from the start when I brought him to the arena on an otherwise calm, warm day. I'm not sure what was going on other than separation from his main equine buddy, Kacee. He acted as if his full-time job was keeping track of her, and he preferred to be very close to her. One could say he found a sense of safety when with her. Knowing these two horses, I'd say her presence regulated him, and that he experienced profound distress when apart from her.

For my own sense of safety, I wanted to do some groundwork with him before I rode, but that quickly became a mess—his attention was with Kacee, not with my requests to walk in a circle. I felt uneasy so I removed his halter and turned him loose in the arena after saddling him, hoping he would run around and blow off some steam. Instead, he bit at the lead rope I was holding, snatching one end of it, and then started flinging his head—and the rope— around. I let go of my end before he took the slack out between us, saving myself from another one of those surprise injuries that occur when we're holding on tight to anything connected to a large, strong animal moving fast. Then he frightened himself as the rope flew around and around his head, as he flung his head around and around with it gripped in his teeth. He reared and struck out with his front legs at the rope. By then I just wanted to get away. I was scared and wanting to protect myself, and wanted to protect him too by not succumbing to my old habit of getting mad at him for scaring me.

I didn't get mad, but I did remain scared until I got the halter on him, which flipped a switch in his brain and allowed me to be more effective in communicating about my personal space. He listened to me when he wore a halter. This had happened before. I knew from prior experience that I could not effectively communicate my boundaries without halter and lead rope when he was that wound up. We have confronted each other in the past, and I would have hoped this feeling between us was resolved, dissolved, gone, but the accidental episode with the lead rope seemed to have triggered his notion that I was confronting him. I was not—but the darn lead rope was. I wasn't ready to consider that something more subtle, such as my mood, was a factor.

When I asked him to walk with me around the arena, he wanted to hang out close to Kacee. His attention was with her, not me. I remembered one of my horsemanship teachers, Harry Whitney, talking about using frequent transitions to draw a horse's mind to you, so I asked Rusty to move off with me in a fast walk, then a trot, then walk, then change directions, and off again with me in a trot. He bolted from me a couple of times, one time which took the lead from me, and another where I was able to stay with him, stumbling, running, trying my best not to slam him in the face with the halter when all the slack threatened to come out of the lead rope, as he was moving faster than I was.

His mood started to change. He softened and was listening better even though I might not have been listening better. I was ready to mount. But he was reluctant to come to the mounting block, stopping a few yards away as I was leading him there. I vaguely registered his opinion, but overrode my timid inner voice and proceeded to get on as if we both felt safe together.

Next came "The Big Three Bs" of Broncing: Bouncing, Bounding, and Bucking. What I did differently that day was to ask him to move out more. "Okay, Rusty. You got some extra energy? Let's go then, let's go!" And go we did.

Bronc Ride Breakthrough #1: I now know I can ride all the various moves he has to offer. Yes, I had one hand on the horn and one hand on the cantle, but at one point I considered proceeding without the two-handed-grasp approach to riding. And yes, I questioned my long-held commitment to encouraging his self-expression in my quest to help him feel confident about offering me his life energy.

Bronc Ride Breakthrough #2: I know I can ride those tight corners, those sudden brakes, those bursts of forward energy. But why do I do this? So I can at least have confidence that my fears will not get in the way of this big-hearted, athletic doll of a horse. As a horse person, this is one of the core things I can do to earn my next ride. The creators of horses have generously given us some who are content offering a lazy ol' time of it, calm in the arena, relaxed on the trails, content to carry a human where the human wants to go. Rusty was not one of those gems.

We got through these outbursts, and I thought about calling it a day, but then thought, "Hey, why stop here? Maybe if I ride him more now, we'll find something else." Plus, I wanted to see if I could help him stretch out his stride, see if all that galloping and gallivanting around helped free him up physically as well as mentally.

So, I asked for trotting when I was doing an activity I call "Find

Something Else" (liven up please when we're headed to where you want to go, chill out when we're headed anyplace else). And when his trot was as usual (short-strided *and* choppy *and* half-hearted) I asked him for more effort. We ended up cantering around and around, sometimes in quite small circles. He still wanted to be near the gate closest to where Kacee was turned out, and I was still practicing *not* steering the direction, just influencing the speed and gait.

Bronc Ride Breakthrough #3: At some point with all this cantering, something shifted. I felt his canter become smoother, easier to sit. At first I thought, "Hey, I'm getting the hang of letting my hips and legs go with his canter motion." Which might have been true. But when it happened again, that feeling of smooth movement under me, I realized it was a change in how he was moving. Why call it "my" breakthrough when truly it was his, as well? His for offering something different, mine for recognizing it.

I was so pleased with this change, with his part of the breakthrough—his letting go somehow in his body and mind—that when he slowed down I hopped off, and that was it for our ride. I rewarded his change with a rest, a break from our riding activities, a time to settle. I left things in a good place, as some of my teachers have advised.

Bronc Ride Breakthrough #4: When I dismounted and loosened his girth, I noticed how heavily he was breathing. I would have liked to have been aware of this while riding, but that would be a project for another ride. Rusty had had a workout. How novel—to ride him hard enough to stress his breathing like that. He wasn't gasping for air or anything, just breathing hard. Breathing hard like that is necessary to get improved cardiovascular fitness. This was a good thing. This is what needed to happen to get him more physically fit—a nice complement to his natural athleticism.

I was pretty excited about all these good things. And I still yearned to just be able to mount up and go for a trail ride like I could on Soli, our older, quiet-minded Haflinger. I'm confident that will be within our comfort zone someday.

OLLIE AND CHIP

I was hired to help a dozen teenage girls learn to get along. They were also being helped by Ollie, who was learning to be a therapy horse. Dappled gray and huge and moderately clueless about turning and stopping, Ollie knew more about socializing than the teenagers did. That was his best attribute. He was an easygoing fellow, happy to hang out with anyone who took him to graze on the lawn, happy to be led around in the arena, circling cones and stepping over ground poles.

Those teenagers loved him because some of his behaviors could be interpreted as affection and liking the girls, and that meant a lot to them. They had been failed in most relationships—at home, at school, in their community. They knew little of safety and trust, of friendship, of getting along. And there was Ollie, humongous and mellow, ready to come in close and nuzzle you. He was probably looking for treats, but the girls didn't know that. They keyed in on being approached by this monstrously large, friendly animal. Ollie provided reparative relationship moments for these youngsters. A little fear (who wouldn't be a little scared of someone that big?) was dissolved by a lot of gentle attention. Plus, this big Ollie animal would go where they asked him to go. Someone was listening to their requests.

Many of the girls who loved Ollie wanted to ride him. Only one wanted to ride him more than once. After noticing this pattern of one ride being enough, I became curious, and realized I needed to ride Ollie myself. I needed to know kinesthetically what was happening while riding him.

Riding Ollie was unpleasant and challenged my balance. I hadn't known the consequence to a human body of sitting on this very awkward, broad-backed, gaited horse who had little understanding of what's expected when being ridden. Ollie's habit was to walk fast in a straight line. He traveled on autopilot and that quality was complicated by something that felt like a hitch in his walk.

After I got off, I asked one of the girls to lead him while I observed.

Ollie did a strange thing. When moving in an arc, most horses will lead with the inside front leg stepping slightly in the direction of the arc. This is how horses easily maintain balance while turning. Ollie did something else. He stepped toward the outside of the arc with his inside front foot. No wonder he felt all wiggly-wobbly to ride. He was unbalanced and that made him feel insecure. His lack of balance also made the rider—way up high on his back—feel unbalanced and insecure. Imagine riding an athletic, inebriated walrus. The memory makes my stomach clench.

Chip, on the other hand, was a therapy horse that everyone wanted to ride again and again. He was ancient in horse years—so old he lived on soaked mash three times a day because his teeth were gone. He liked to gum hay and was smart enough to drop it from his mouth rather than try to swallow the big, wet wads. He was predictably a slow mover and his preferred speed was a full stop. He was shorter than many horses, so the distance to the ground was less frightening for those who rode him. The problem was he was so old that he was officially retired from riding. His back had sunk into the conformation we call swaybacked, and we were unsure if he was comfortable carrying a saddle and rider.

It was a challenge for us staff to say no to the girls who wanted to ride, and only wanted to ride Chip. Saying no often triggered their protest in the form of raging tantrums targeted at us adults. In face of the conflict between protecting Chip and protecting ourselves, we usually protected Chip. As it can be with horse people, we often choose to take care of our horses instead of ourselves.

Sadly, these girls, as much as they were attracted to the horses, hadn't developed those empathy parts, the parts that can care more about the welfare of another than one's own yearnings. I understood their wanting to be close to Chip. He was a safe being for them. He was disabled by age. They were disabled by social circumstances and all the developmental delays and losses that come from abuse and neglect in families and schools. Chip was an ally. Chip was a compadre. Chip was a confidant. Chip stuck around when a trickle of tears was allowed in the privacy of leaning into the mane of a just-right-sized horse. Being with Chip was the first time it felt safe to be vulnerable. Being with Chip was a gateway to hope for something more.

When I'm Scared

The sympathetic nervous system's flight or fight response is just as normal as all the other survival responses that show up. If I perceive something as threatening, I prepare to survive by moving away from the threat (flight) or overcoming it (fight).

Both fight and flight involve energy and focus; indeed, our eyes take on a focused state so that we can more clearly see the escape route, or the enemy we will battle. In this state, when we are focused, it's much harder to keep track of what's in our peripheral vision—the bigger picture of what's happening. This could be the actual bigger picture of what and who are where in our environment. This also could mean the bigger picture of why I became sympathetically activated and what my survival options are.

Regarding vision and states, it's a two-way street. When the sympathetic nervous system is activated, our focal vision is dominant. Likewise, when I'm visually focused on something, my sympathetic system gets activated.

It is physiologically hard to keep track of the big picture when we've narrowed in on an immediate danger or are in a state of fear. Focused vision—convergence—triggers this sympathetic activation, which is designed for fixating on a potential threat and readying for action. Peripheral vision—divergence—triggers parasympathetic arousal, eliciting a calming effect.

We can intentionally shift vergence—how we focus—and shift autonomic nervous system states. One way to shift from sympathetic to parasympathetic is by shifting our visual orientation from convergence to divergence. We can do that on purpose—looking away from a stressful focal point to the calming horizon—to downshift from a more sympathetically aroused state.

It's easy to get mad at ourselves, as if we have control over the triggers and our responses. This was the case when I was riding Kacee. She got upset, which scared me, and in turn I scared her with my behavior and the force of my emotions. Then of course one of us had to downshift and by doing so help the other downshift. And in this particular interspecies relationship—between horse and human—it's the human's responsibility to seek a settled, regulated state and help the horse settle.

It took me years of triggering Rusty before I learned to put off going to the barn when I had any inkling that I was upset about anything in my life. For a while, it was quite usual for me to be upset with my then-husband and seek comfort—or at least distraction from my anger—by going to the barn to do something with my horses. Kacee could tolerate my moods, and I have some theories as to why she could and why Rusty couldn't. My internal discordant, wound-up state was enough to upset Rusty without my ever even saying or doing anything.

My thoughts about why Kacee could while Rusty couldn't? I look to their earliest days. Kacee was born in a field and was basically an unhandled horse for the first months of her life. No restraints, no stalls, no humans pushing or pulling on her. She moved, she rested, she nursed, she nibbled, she ran full steam whenever she felt the desire to. She did not experience the developmental challenges that Rusty did. Rusty was born in a stall and his mother was removed from the stall when he was three months old. He continued to live in that stall until I bought him and took him home when he was a yearling.

Horses are mentally, emotionally, socially, and physically impaired by being denied access to space and contact and interactions with their own species. Rusty lived in a chronic highly activated sympathetic state, frequently becoming immobilized in freeze, and sometimes tipping into the shutdown state of collapse.

Ollie and Chip were an interesting contrast of fear and confusion versus confidence and trust. Also interesting were the troubled youth drawn to Ollie, themselves living with fear and confusion underneath whatever adaptive skills they'd learned and could access.

There are always life events that trigger higher levels of sympathetic activation. It could be driving on ice and losing traction for a second. It could be watching a toddler lose balance and land with a thump on the floor. It could be reading the latest news about war horrors, or when a picture of your least favorite political leader pops up on your social media newsfeed. It could be walking along the edge of a field on a sunny afternoon and being surprised by a snake napping on a rock.

What I wonder is how easily we can shift. Does it take days of worry and telling friends about the snake or the toddler falling before I start to feel like myself again? Or does it take minutes? These things reflect my baseline autonomic nervous system physiology and how resilient I am—how easy it is to shift states according to changes in my actual safety.

Once Ollie scared the girls, they wanted to have little to do with him. One infraction, one upset, and their trust dissolved. They didn't know (yet) how to process the upset and regain the trust. Chip, on the other hand, did not challenge their trust.

I think trust needs to be challenged at times so we can learn to repair relationships after feelings have been upset. Those girls in residential treatment needed on-call 24/7 help to learn these things. And still it was slow. But repair with oneself, and repair with others (horses and humans alike) are both possible. We can build the bridges to feeling safe again. Or in some cases, build the bridges to start to connect with the possibility of feeling safe. Those girls with Ollie and Chip, and horses like Rusty, did not have the early experiences of connection and feeling safe that Kacee and many people have. I'm a firm believer that although some of us will never be as whole and at ease as those who started with a base of safe relationships, we can keep getting better and better—healing and growing our capacity for feeling secure—as long as we are alive.

CHAPTER 6

Immobilization

Not all stillness is calm. — Sarah Schlote

His brain has learned that trying doesn't work, that nothing he does makes a difference ... and so he has lost the ability to try.
— Emily Nagoski and Amelia Nagoski

Scared and Alone

Each year, the Moffats, owners of the local stables where I started taking riding lessons when I was seven, lent out some of their horses to be kept and enjoyed for the late fall, winter, and spring months at no charge. I was That Horse Crazy Girl, The Kid Who Will Do Anything to Be Near Horses, and earned the Moffats' respect during my time in lessons and helping with barn chores. That meant I was allowed to take home of one of their horses for the off-season. I spent three years doing this, simultaneously proving to my parents that I could and would take on the responsibilities that come with owning a horse.

The first year I had Half Moon, a big, easygoing black and white pinto. The second year it was Sammy, a smaller, very tolerant roan pony. My best friend and I regularly made up circus tricks, fell off, and lay giggling at his feet in puddles of silliness. Tag Me, a kindly buckskin, was my horse the third year. He was special because I'd named him, winning a Name the New Horse contest at the stables.

I don't recall the prize but I remember how pleased I was to have Tag Me at home with me.

One evening I was doing barn chores after a ride. Tag Me stood tied, still wearing his saddle. I mucked his box stall, filled his water bucket, and was dropping a bale of hay from the loft when he slipped out of his halter and ambled through the open barn doors. I panicked. My horse was loose and I didn't know how I would catch him and bring him back into the barn. It was dark out—and it would be many years before we would have the convenience of calling for help with a cell phone. I hurried down from the loft and out the door after him, grabbing hold of the only thing he was wearing, his saddle. I stood there, heart pounding, hoping he would stay put. I knew full well I was incapable of stopping him if he chose to walk off. It was 900-pound horse versus 100-pound kid who didn't have a halter or a lead rope, or anybody around to help.

Despite my panic, Tag Me seemed content. He wasn't trying to get away from me. He wasn't disappearing into the acres and acres of fields and woods surrounding our home. But I didn't fully believe that he wasn't going to run off. I was terrified of losing him, and I was alone. Standing there, heart aching, with aching fingers still grasping the saddle, I sobbed. He stayed. He stayed near while I melted into this gripping fear. And something came alive in me, some gut sense of having an unnamed need met. He stayed even though I was out of my mind with panic.

I think I called out to my parents, but I'm not sure. This memory is mixed with one of my recurring nightmares—the one where I'm trying to cry for help but no sound comes. All this effort, every cell in my body screaming, but no sound comes. So maybe I called for help. Nobody heard me, though. It was close to suppertime and the TV was probably on with Mom cooking, Dad in his study, and my older brother setting the table. The house seemed an inaccessible distance from where I stood outside the barn. Probably I didn't call out for help, discouraged into silent failure before I even tried.

My eyes ran, my nose ran, I gasped for breath between sobs.

I held on to Tag Me's saddle. As my anguish started to subside, I remembered his saddle had stirrup leathers that I could remove and buckle around his neck, and maybe with those I could lead him back into the barn. Tentatively I proceeded, fearful he would walk off at any point. There was so much I didn't know about horses and relationships. So much I wasn't prepared for. But I did it anyway. I unbuckled a stirrup leather and pulled it loose from the saddle. I placed it over his neck and buckled it under his throat. With one hand on this makeshift lead rope, I led him back into the barn.

I closed the barn door. He couldn't leave again. My tears dried and my shoulders stopped shaking as I took off his saddle and put him in his stall with his evening hay. I turned off the lights and headed to the house, entering just as Mom was putting supper on the table. Nobody noticed the remnants of my distress: swollen eyes, furrowed brow, slumped posture. Nobody asked how I was doing. Life went on as if this near disaster—which felt like a disaster—had not happened. My belly still felt knotted, but that didn't stop me from sitting down to dinner. I hadn't yet learned to speak up when not asked, to let people know when I was in distress. That came much later in life.

That winter with Tag Me marked my passing some invisible test my parents had set. I had proved my dedication to horse care for three years. This horse attraction wasn't a whim. I was granted permission to own a horse.

Bridling Rusty

I could always bridle Rusty, sooner or later. I preferred to do it alone with him with no onlookers. This was easy when I was at home. In horsemanship clinic settings, where I spent much of my riding time with him, I told myself I needed to be alone with him so I could focus and relax. The truth was that the process of bridling him was messy and I didn't want anyone to see. I got frustrated and it always took at least ten tries before I could get the bit in his mouth. And those words describe my attitude—I was intent on getting something done, on making him do what I wanted him to do.

When he had been younger, I set out to bridle him like I bridled other horses. I was baffled that it didn't work. I went to clinics and mimicked all the great horsemen I could study with. That didn't work either. I would bring the bridle and Rusty would lift his head. I would stand on a mounting block so I could reach as high as he could lift his head, and he would swing his head away from me. Or, worse, he would swing his head into me, knocking me off balance and off the mounting block. I would try to hold his head in place. He would lift me off my feet. He was stronger than I was, even if I was strong enough to hold on.

One year at a horsemanship clinic with Mark Rashid, I had enough courage to go public with this mess. I led Rusty haltered to our lesson, his bridle hanging from the saddle horn.

"I think I need help. Bridling isn't going as nice as I think it could."

Mark responded, "I see you have your bridle with you. Do what you usually do and we'll see what's happening." Mark watched as Rusty and I did our bridling fiasco. My bridling efforts again and again resulted in me frustrated and Rusty without a bridle. Mark gently spoke up again. "If you don't mind, can I try something?"

"Please," I said as a few tears seeped up from my aching heart and out my eyes.

I can't tell you what Mark did. I was standing there with my eyes open but much of me was collapsed in shame, not only for this mess but also because I felt so exposed in my frustration and ineptness. Mark bridled Rusty after a few tries which started out looking like my dance with Rusty but quickly morphed. Mark's dance with Rusty was smooth and successful on the bridling front. Looking back, I suspect Mark was bringing his high-level ability to remain deep-to-the-core calm to this little maelstrom I'd created with Rusty. Rusty and I were used to engaging in a certain way, and from what I learned from Mark, Rusty was just doing what he thought I wanted, even though it felt as bad to him as it did to me. Mark was offering this calmness while also doing this bridling activity, and Rusty found his way to being calm while accepting the bit. After my years of dancing with Rusty, it took only a few minutes for Rusty to learn a new dance. Same bridle, same bit—different people, different presentations. Rusty had an easy yes to Mark's request.

I practiced there under Mark's keen eye and kind tutelage until Rusty had an easy yes to my request. He yawned a lot and his eyes rolled back and he shook his head and neck, actions I recognized as ways that horses tell us, "Wow, doing this with you feels so much better now." More waves of shame passed through me—about making life so unpleasant for Rusty as well as for not having known before how to bridle this particular horse. Those feelings were mixed with a little terror, thinking I would not be able to keep this up on my own after the clinic.

Indeed, the tests came time and time again after that clinic. I called them "tests" because with Rusty, I had to bring forth my most centered, balanced, calm state. I'd been testing myself, "Can I be the person Rusty needs me to be?" Many times, yes. Sometimes, no. But I learned that bridling Rusty wasn't about the bit; it was about how I presented it to him. My presence. My vibe. My autonomic nervous system state, which I had hoped was that of relaxed engagement. And my comfort, as I persisted without hurry, to join with him in a place of soft togetherness.

Hard to Be Here

After getting fitted for a helmet, Willa stood stock still facing the shelves full of toys—beanbags, miniature plastic horses, transformer robots, and colorful foam balls the size of grapefruits. She had arrived a few minutes earlier for her weekly lesson, which would include talking, expressive arts, and horse time as part of the equine-assisted mental health program I had developed.

"It's time to go to my office, Willa." She lowered her head and looked sideways at her aunt, wordlessly begging to play with the toys. "Looks like you want to bring a toy with you today?" She nodded yes to my question, still sending begging vibes to her aunt. Her aunt looked at me. I looked at Willa. "Okay. Choose one toy to bring with you."

Willa picked up one toy, then another, and then another. "I want this one."

"Okay."

"Uh, I want this one."

"Hmmm, one toy, Willa. Which one do you want today?"

We bargained for five minutes until Willa chose the red and silver transformer robot, then we headed to my office where I'd set up a box of crayons and five pieces of paper. Being clear about limits was part of my responsibility in our relationship, and I was feeling uncertain about how I was doing—that dance between being kind and understanding, and sticking to a limit I'd set.

Before going to live with her aunt, Willa had experienced physical and emotional abuse by her parents. Early trauma created deep wounds and disrupted her natural inclination to trust. Here she was at five years old, one of the walking wounded, a survivor living in alternating states of terror and collapse, with too few of those management skills many of us older walking wounded have acquired. Adults with clear boundaries, consistency, and kindness are key for a child to develop a sense of trust and safety. And for one hour each week, I was that adult who might make a difference.

Our lesson plan started with drawing and play in my office, followed by time outside, where Willa would learn riding skills and relating skills, whether with horses or the volunteers.

Willa entered the office and sat down, eyeing the crayons and paper, and froze. Her eyes were wide and gazing off to some place far away that I imagined was safer than here. "What colors do you like, Willa? You get to choose. And you can draw whatever you like." I wanted to relieve her of any compulsion to do it right or perfectly, and let her just draw, which would give me hints about

IMMOBILIZATION

what she sees and feels and can't put into words. I didn't even notice I hadn't offered her the choice to color or not.

She opened the box and dumped the crayons onto the table, glancing at me to see my response. I smiled. I consciously exhaled. I was fine with what she'd done and wanted to convey that with my breathing. Some part of her registered when someone was breathing or holding their breath. She started to crayon. I watched as her hand grasped the orange crayon and pressed into the paper, breaking the tip off of that crayon, then the red crayon, then the black. That much pressure was what felt right, and out onto the paper came colors, chaos, fire.

Then she pushed aside the crayons and focused on the toy she'd chosen. "That was sudden, Willa. Anything you'd like to say about being done with coloring?" She gave no sign of hearing me as I spoke.

Playing with this toy appeared urgent. In Willa's hands, the transformer became a killer robot. It attacked me, the table, the walls. The robot battled with Willa's imaginary enemies. At one point I prompted her to ask her aunt for help to feel safe with all these scary things happening. Willa went to her and leaned in, looking herself like a rigid robot transformer despite the warmth offered. The behaviors of safety didn't connect her to a new experience of melting into feeling safe. Feeling safe wasn't part of her experience.

It was time to head to the riding ring for her horse time. On our way there, Willa squatted and drew her fingers through the sand, creating picture stories as she did with the crayons and the robot, stories that she couldn't put into words. Her actions said she wanted more self-directed play time before greeting the volunteers and her horse Misty. I was curious about her need to delay engaging. Was she integrating her office time, or dissociating as she went into these imaginary stories? Dissociation was a very important coping strategy for her, as it is for all of us. *I can be here doing this if I'm also not here doing this.*

Once Willa got to the ring, she mounted and smiled, patting

Misty's neck while the volunteers led them around the ring. When Willa picked up the reins and practiced steering, Misty braced against the reins and Willa's comfort vanished.

Willa yelled. "Misty is naughty! She hates me!"

I stepped in to be close. "You're upset that she didn't listen to your request?"

Misty's own willfulness—or perhaps misunderstanding of what Willa wanted—devastated Willa, whose trust in any horse or human was tentative at best. She disappeared behind defensiveness and dissociation, covering where vulnerability felt threatening. Misty walking straight when Willa wanted to turn was a betrayal that triggered the wordless helplessness and rage and terror and sorrow that waited inside.

As the instructor, I adjusted the lesson plan to allow for Willa's emotions to surface and settle. She rode without using the reins while the volunteer led, and her large sympathetic activation started to subside. Willa was returning to her comfort zone after her big upset. No shaming her for the outburst, just offering a break from the stimulus that was overwhelming. That was my priority. Then to mediate her relationship with Misty, I demonstrated how to verbalize emotions, using words to express being mad, disappointed, scared, and pleased. And I wondered to myself whether being carried by the horse was more important right then than learning to direct the horse or learning how to use words to express feelings.

Being heard was important to Willa. It was intolerable when Misty didn't do what was asked. Willa shifted from being collapsed before riding, to being mildly engaged while riding, to being furious when Misty didn't do what Willa wanted. Willa's infant part was showing up to say, "Listen to me! I can't survive if you don't do what I want! I'm devastated when you don't meet my needs: when you don't see me, hear me, or come to me! I am helpless and need to know you will respond to me!"

I felt my own heartaches surfacing. The pain of misattunement. The despair of being a child in a world of adults who weren't responding to my signal cries. The loneliness. The unfathomable rage that a young body can barely tolerate. The fear of more pain, living side by side with tidbits of hope that *this time it will be different*.

Recovery Not Guaranteed

Rusty stepped on my toe. It was evening feeding time, and as I entered his run-in shed with an armful of hay he backed into me, letting me know he had some itches between his hind legs needing my immediate attention. I wasn't prepared for this—wasn't paying attention—and lost my balance, starting to fall backwards. As I was righting myself, he continued back, this time landing on my foot. The comfortable neoprene boots that keep the mud, manure, and other dirt and wet stuff away from my feet and socks did nothing to protect me from Rusty's weight. I yelled at him as I dropped the hay, leaned into his rump, and pushed him away. My belly churned with the pain as I moaned, limping toward the barn, leaving the rest of the chores to my partner Terry.

Months later I could still see the mark where the blood blister was growing out under my big toenail. It no longer hurt, but I was still wary around Rusty. When big animals hurt us, it takes time to recover trust. The trust I needed wasn't just trust in Rusty, but trust in myself. I didn't trust that I could avoid being hurt again. I needed to practice being alert to my surroundings at every moment, especially around horses. That would be one way I could build trust in my ability to keep myself safe and protect myself from injury in the future.

One of my therapeutic riding students was practicing keeping her balance while riding Edie, a stocky draft pony, during walk-trot-walk transitions. Leading Edie was a kind and talented volunteer named Ryan who was practicing something he'd learned in an Advanced Leader Training I'd taught for our program volunteers. He was leading Edie with some slack in the lead rope. This allows for more space between the leader and the horse, and lets the horse move forward with its natural straightness through the head, neck, and shoulders. Without slack in the lead rope, the horse's head is drawn to the left where the leader is often holding tight in hopes of controlling the horse.

My horsemanship teachers have helped me see something about the horses' ability to learn and their readiness to get along with others. When I teach leading skills to volunteers, I want them to experience for themselves what a horse is capable of understanding and doing, like following the pace and direction of the leader even without a lead rope. Many times I've seen the surprise of accomplished horsepersons in their volunteer roles when they first experience leading a horse with slack in the lead rope.

I was at the far end of the arena and called out for them to trot. As Edie started to trot, Ryan shortened his grasp on the lead rope. I said nothing, hesitant to micromanage his leading in the middle of a lesson. Then Edie stepped on his foot.

There are numerous stresses during the actual lessons that I'm sure contributed to this return of old leading habits. Many of us learned that keeping a lead rope taut is how to be safe around horses. So we had a scenario in the lesson where the newer learnings (slack in the lead rope) slipped into the background when stress was high, and the prior lessons learned—the habits—returned. When Ryan became stressed while leading Edie, his grip tightened. Edie became a little off-balance as she started trotting because she didn't have the freedom to swing her head and neck normally. Then she stepped in toward Ryan, yielding to pressure as we want our horses to do, and landed on his foot, something we don't want our horses to do.

A shower of pain and blame ensued. Ryan blamed himself for messing up during a lesson. He blamed me for asking him to move into a trot. In my thoughts, I blamed Ryan for not giving Edie enough lead rope to allow her to trot in balance. I worried about the extent of Ryan's injuries and felt guilty that he was hurt during my lesson. Nobody was feeling good about what had happened, including our volunteer coordinator, who blamed me for failing to keep Ryan safe. The incident also affected the rider whose lesson was interrupted as we tended to Ryan's injury—and Edie, who felt our vibes of discord.

Knowing how much a painful memory lingers and interferes with the feeling of safety, peace, and harmony between two mammals, I could understand our various reactions even as I wished none of this had happened. It's a wild card whether we ever recover our willingness to be close to whomever upset us. I have a lifelong commitment to my horse Rusty, and most of the time my love is greater than my fear. Sadly, that was not the case with this volunteer, who did not return to my lessons after his foot healed. The incident caused a relationship rupture we didn't know how to repair.

Immobilization

When neither fight nor flight is possible, collapse happens—the automatic go-to of an overwhelmed nervous system that has no other survival strategy options. This energy-conserving state looks a lot like a very calm state, but it is not. Heart rate is slowed, as is breathing rate, in a layered experience. On the outside we appear calm, while inside our life energy is crazy wild chaos under lockdown.

Collapse is the most challenging of our autonomic states for me to write about. I'm familiar with it. I've been comfortable in the immobilization of collapse despite my ideas of what I prefer: energetic, engaged, and productive. When feeling threatened, I seldom flee or fight. Every cell of my body knows I collapsed and survived in infancy, so it became the first survival strategy my autonomic nervous system employs. This automatic response involves homeostasis which, if it could speak, would say, "What happened then to keep me alive was successful, so don't you dare try to change anything."

Many of us have grown up in chronic partially immobilized states of freeze and/or collapse since early in life. Before muscles and coordination developed, we were physically incapable of moving toward a safe person or fleeing or fighting when we felt threatened. The threat could have been from something as benign as loud noises, or as invasive as life-saving medical interventions. We could not mobilize but, like Willa and many infants, we survived infancy anyway. Willa's signal cries got no response, her emotional and attachment needs were not met, and she carried the ensuing wounds. Infants need to get their needs met by reliable adult caregivers responding to their signal cries. For infants, it can be perceived as a life-or-death situation. Instead of actually dying, they collapse and dissociate.

How do we tell the difference between a true sense of calm and the many faces of partial collapse and partial freeze—such as compliant, yielding, dead broke, bombproof, obedient, dull, withdrawn, unresponsive, spaced out? It is not always easy. When Tag Me walked out of the barn, I went into a partial collapse. I could go to him and hold onto his saddle (not collapsed) but I couldn't call for help (collapsed) and my problem solving (realizing I could use a stirrup leather to lead him) was compromised (collapsed).

Willa was living with the nervous system of an abused and neglected infant even though her current living circumstances were safe. Little of the love and kindness offered her was allowed entry past her internal protective parts. She did not know she was safe, welcome, and valued. She harbored an insatiable hole of fear and isolation and was practiced at avoiding any of the feelings that lurked there. I honored her need to avoid—it was key to her survival at that point. And I hoped she would have experiences with horses and with our therapeutic team that would feel safe enough to create an entryway for nourishment to sink in and start healing her insides.

Living in a state of suspended development haunts people through life unless interventions start installing the missing pieces. Healing gets harder and harder as a child grows physically; adults expect more controlled, thoughtful behaviors from older children. Willa was marginally capable on the best of days, but

IMMOBILIZATION

she tried her hardest. Like me, and like her aunt, she wanted to feel safe, she wanted to belong. I didn't always have words for this when I worked with her, but I felt it in my bones and offered what I could to change the trajectory of her life.

In the horsemanship clinic setting, I had needed the support of Mark Rashid's calm presence to shift my state in order to bridle Rusty. Mark stood quietly—speaking in soothing tones—and waited during my confession: I had been hiding in the past when I bridled Rusty (collapsed state). I had felt Mark attentive with every cell in his body as I exposed my struggles (high sympathetic state), then I proceeded to learn how to bridle Rusty without those struggles (engaged and feeling safe enough). In the therapeutic riding lesson, after Edie stepped on the volunteer's foot, I wasn't able to be that necessary calm presence for the volunteer or the volunteer coordinator. All three of us were in a state of high sympathetic activation. My own upset turned to helplessness as I watched relationship ruptures unfold within the team.

When that state of upset and high activation persists for too long, it can lead to the immobilization we call burnout—in horses as well as people. My desire to reduce burnout in therapy horses is what motivated me to start writing this book. I wanted those horses to stay engaged and content with their work. Then, I expanded to wanting to avoid burnout for people as well as for horses.

Burnout is the result of living with more distress than enjoyment. When we're giving more than we're getting and spending more time pleasing others than taking care of our own needs, we are at risk for burnout. We shut down when we are chronically misunderstood or criticized, and when we are not allowed to contribute or have an opinion but are only expected to do what someone else tells us to do.

As I write about this, I can feel how burnout shows up in my body, emotions, and thoughts. I feel heavy, sitting a bit slumped in my chair. I lose interest in what I'm doing. I stare into space more than usual. Thoughts of "why bother" and "who cares" predominate.

With horses, burnout can be precipitated by chronic boredom, social isolation, lack of understanding of what's expected, or exposure to too many new people, places, or things. Some horses will nip or kick in an effort to get away from job stress, pain, or confinement. Some horses can't get away and move into partial immobilization. The urge to flee from threat is thwarted and turns into collapse. *I have no control over my environment.*

The horses with pinned ears and dull eyes—the ones we call cranky, stubborn, lazy, or sour? Do we notice these bigger signs of discontent even if we may misinterpret them? These horses lack enthusiasm. They are only marginally willing to engage with us. What about the smaller signs, the horse's more subtle responses to inescapable, stressful circumstances? What can we do to notice these changes in their prodromal stages—those things that happen before something else happens? Can we interrupt the progression to burnout?

We don't want to keep missing the little things that make a difference.

CHAPTER 7

Emerging from Immobilization

———————— ⚘ ————————

You don't realize how much effort you've put into covering things up until you try to dig them out. — LILY KING

If you want to improve the world, start by making people feel safer. — STEPHEN W. PORGES

EXPECTING TOO MUCH

I WAS A STUDENT in a horsemanship clinic in Arizona with a borrowed horse called Charlie, and I was stuck. I had wanted to finish something I'd started—intent on doing things my way. I had insisted Charlie do what I asked regardless of what he could actually understand or how he was feeling in that moment. I had forgotten this whole notion of prioritizing how to help my horse feel better.

Our morning ride had gone well in the familiar confines of the large sandy arena. Charlie and I had been getting acquainted, even as my attention strayed at times from our walk and trot transitions to beyond the arena, where clusters of saguaros punctuated the otherwise monotonous terrain. After lunch, together with seven other horses and riders from the clinic and our clinician, Harry Whitney, we went for a ride on a trail crisscrossed by arroyos, those dry creek beds left after a deluge of desert rainfall.

Toward the end of the ride, I steered Charlie off the trail away from the main group, toward where Harry was sitting tall but relaxed on his horse, the two meandering along among the dry brush. I was keen to talk with him about horsemanship. Charlie grew up-headed and antsy, and I grew firmer with the reins, tightening my breath as well as my hands. I intended to communicate, "Let go of your idea and slow down, please." I misread the extent of his anxiety—we were too far from the rest of the horses, in his opinion. By now I was busy managing my own anxieties about riding a worried horse (*Would he explode? Would I be launched onto a cactus?*) and about being in full view of Harry's all-seeing eyes and experienced perspective. I was so focused on my little plan, it hadn't occurred to me to give up my idea of riding with Harry in order to try something else, like something geared to help Charlie feel better about being out in the desert, separated from his herd.

Harry offered a couple of suggestions. Take a shortcut to catch up with the group. Trot to catch up with them. Simple stuff that would have let Charlie know I understood his survival impulses were so big he couldn't listen to my directions right then. I chose to take the shortcut, not daring to let him trot.

At the end of that clinic day—as horses settled in their paddocks and humans gathered at the dinner table—I braved asking Harry about what had happened. We talked about my narrow-mindedness when riding Charlie that afternoon. Harry asked if I would expect a kid to know it all right away. And my answer was yes, confirming my outlandish expectations. I had forgotten how little this dear old horse Charlie knew. He was a kid in elementary school. I had forgotten that our three days together wasn't enough time to enable us to hear each other when stressed. And stress was rampant that afternoon. I stressed him by not listening to him. I stressed him by shouting through the reins when he couldn't hear my whispers. I was stressed by his not responding exactly as I'd wanted. I was stressed by sitting atop a very worried horse.

I had expected too much of Charlie. I hadn't been able to access any creative problem-solving thoughts about helping him feel better. I had forgotten how little he knew about me and whether I was worth listening to. And I was mad at myself, and ashamed. For expecting what worked in the arena to work on the trail. For my failure to hear his nervous system and his lack of readiness to take direction. I had been stuck on my plan. I was upset with Charlie who'd needed the support of his horse friends. It had not been a good idea to argue with this worried horse about who was going to yield.

That talk with Harry haunted me. It called me to face my failings. Why couldn't I access some creativity or even some other solutions? Where had my brain gone? And I felt so sad, missing this chance to support a horse in need. Ashamed of my deficiency, I ached with wanting to be better at this. To be fairer and have a better understanding of horses.

It was shocking to recognize this gap between what I could mentally grasp about horses and how I actually behaved when with them.

Catching My Breath

One of my favorite Somatic Experiencing® Practitioners worked in an old brick building that housed a maze of long narrow hallways opening into small rooms with tall windows. Coming into her office, I heard the clank and hiss of the cast-iron radiator as we greeted each other with a hug. I'd been looking forward to her hug—warm and soft and present, without lingering, without encapsulation. She settled into her rocking chair across from the small armchair where I sat. I rearranged the pillows behind my back until my body felt supported and I started to relax. I was there for another Somatic Experiencing® session, one of many required in my three-year professional training.

She was familiar to me as a teaching assistant in my Somatic Experiencing® training, and I already felt safe thanks to her gentle tone of voice, warm smile, and visible radiance that accompanied her every time I saw her.

I never knew what would surface when I went for a session. I did know something would surface, as I had called for this appointment when I noticed myself feeling off—annoyed and complaining about daily life events like doing dishes, driving to work, bringing hay out to the horses and sheep.

"What do you notice in your body as you tell me about the animals crowding you this morning?" Her dark brown eyes were wide with curiosity as she guided my attention to my body sensations. This was a core element in Somatic Experiencing®. This is where we get information from repressed body memories. With preverbal trauma, healing comes not from the stories about what might have happened, but from allowing the body to experience what it became dissociated from in times of overwhelm and in the absence of an engaged, supportive person.

Looking inside with eyes closed, I described what I noticed. "Tight throat, heaviness in my chest, arms kinda dead at my sides."

"Is it okay to stay with these sensations?"

I nodded, thinking to myself, "I can handle whatever happens."

My breathing became shallow and rapid as I sat with my attention on the sensations in my throat and chest as they intensified. My eyes opened and locked on to hers. I could feel her calm presence and at the same time, I could feel what I later would call terror. My breathing became more rapid and high in my chest, shifting into a gasping pattern that wasn't ending. I was scared, and yet there she was and she was not afraid. Something in me thought, "Scary as shit but okay to be this scared." She wasn't worried about me, so I could stop worrying about what was happening and just be with my breathing and terror that was surfacing.

Minutes seemed like hours of gasping. And then it started to change. Smaller gasps, less frequent gasps, settling of the breathing pattern and settling of the terror. All this in silence. This safe capsule of silence where my preverbal experience could surface. Lasting silence as we faced each other, her nervous system offering regulation to my nervous system. My body shuddered and then shuddered again. My body gasped again a few more times. Then my body found a free and easy breathing rhythm, like nothing I'd ever experienced before. When she spoke, it was only to name it. "Your natural breathing."

In my mind I started calling it "baby breathing." This is how babies breathe if they've not been overwhelmed before or during birth. Breath comes in. Breath goes out. Short pause. Breath comes in again. Breath goes out again. Short pause again. No thoughts other than a quiet noting of this breathing pattern. No tension, no worries, no past or future. Just this gentle rise and fall from the inside connected with all of the cells of my body. Peacefulness.

This was a significant moment for me, emerging from a chronic state of partial collapse. That moment built on smaller pieces of somatic work during that training and, in some connected way, throughout my adult years of spiritual and therapeutic adventures. That day, those pieces congealed into a me who felt safe enough to allow that terror to surface, and to allow the freedom that was waiting.

Enthusiasm

Christy arrived for her first lesson sporting new jodhpurs, new paddock boots, and a crisp white long-sleeved shirt. She was wide-eyed and speechless with enthusiasm. As the volunteers fitted her with a riding helmet, her mother told us of her fascination with My Little Pony™. Christy slowed her steps, hesitating as she got close to Jack, her lesson horse. The toy horses and videos had not been enough to prepare her for touching and riding the real live pony that was now in front of her.

The volunteers and I waited as Christy's arousal settled—breathing slowed, fists relaxed, eyes softened—and then we helped her mount. Her body started to grow accustomed to the motion of Jack's walk as he was led forward. Then she adjusted to riding through turns and stops and starts. Each demanded different body parts to cooperate, a dance of flexibility, coordination, and strength. She rode in straight lines as a rest from the physiological stress of riding these other ways. Despite the challenges, her smile radiated out to all of the lesson team.

These transitions were a big deal. I was asking a system that was used to functioning a particular way to do something new, to venture into the unknown. Humans are wired to be alert for danger, and novelty can be perceived as dangerous. Many of us have experiences of getting scared or hurt when trying new things, like the not-so-simple simplest of things when a child starts walking after mastering crawling. Most of us make this transition from crawling to standing to walking. Most of us fall repeatedly while we're figuring out this new relationship with gravity, balancing while in motion. I wonder how many of us bring remnants of these early experiences when we start riding, and even carry them with us through our entire career of riding. Fear of falling lies dormant and can accompany us every time we get on top of a horse.

I was in longtime denial of my own fear as a rider. My friends had watched me ride and cringed, praying I'd stay with the horse and not go flying through the air in a different direction from where the horse was flying through the air. Eventually, I found my way to conscious fear. I'm glad I can say I've survived falls, kicks, being stepped on, being knocked over. I tried harder to ensure the safety of my students than I did my own.

During Christy's later lessons, we played games like toss and catch with small beanbags to help her adjust to balancing while riding. Engaging her hands with something familiar allowed the muscles in her torso to figure out this mounted stuff.

She was ready with a yes to whatever we suggested, even when her brain struggled with how to do new things. I didn't always know how to bridge the gap between what I had in mind and what she could understand, but I imagine I had as much fun learning how to communicate with her as she had progressing from leadline lessons to riding independently.

Christy wasn't aware of fear or how her body responded when scared. I was keen to recognize and honor her body's subtle messages of fear—stiffening, holding breath, eyes widening. This became part of her lesson plan: when she tightened, I would notice it and name it, and guess out loud why. Maybe she hadn't understood a request. Maybe she hadn't felt balanced when holding the reins or moving one hand away from her body to turn the horse.

There are very good reasons why we should be fearful around horses—their size and reactivity mean they can knock us over, step on us, even kick us before we can move to safety. With fear comes alertness, and this can help us keep safe when we're standing near, walking alongside, mounting, riding, or dismounting horses. It's like graduate school for us humans to be able to coexist with love, fear, and action. It's way too easy to freeze when scared—and become immobilized by fear.

Christy had some of these elements of freeze before she started riding. Stiff back. Stiff arms and hands. Stiff legs and hips. Her face revealed little emotional nuance. Her tone of voice, however, expressed more variation than the rest of her body did. Slowly, slowly while riding Jack, fluidity in her joints replaced some of the rigidity. Her body was coming out of freeze. Her confidence grew and her spirit sparkled.

Her family was one hundred percent on board with our lesson plans and shared our excitement about her progress with riding skills. Last I knew, Christy was riding independently at the walk, trot, and canter, and occasionally popping over small jumps. At whatever pace she needed, she learned—and she learned deeply, all the time with a smile on her face.

Emerging from Immobilization

I grew up hearing the expression, "What you don't know won't hurt you." I disagree. I have been haunted by what I didn't know. Those early preverbal memories of birth trauma, buried thanks to the normal physiology of survival, left undercurrents of suppressed fear and mistrust. What was kept hidden defined and confined the scope of my life experiences.

We've all seen a picture of a horse with head up, ears forward, nostrils wide, whole-body tense, eyes focused on something. The horse is orienting to something potentially dangerous as it assesses, "Is this friend or foe?"

When this happens in a herd, the horse takes cues from other horses to either run or settle back to quiet movement or grazing. Too often, we humans haven't earned the trust of horses, so they do not take cues from us about safety, danger, or threat. We humans get scared, and often injured, when horses are taking care of their survival needs without checking in with us.

If the horse's sympathetic mobilization of flight or fight is thwarted, a natural mammalian response is collapse. We might call this a shutdown horse, a dead broke horse, or a dull horse.

Humans and horses go into freeze or collapse from a state of super-high sympathetic activation. To come out of immobilization, we pass through that same super-high sympathetic state. It's the access route to settling toward *genuine calmness* in the nervous system, not to be confused with the *apparent calm* of a partially shutdown horse, or of a human who has given up or been managing upsets with efforts designed to contain strong, unwelcome feelings.

Relying on a safe-enough horse is tempting even if that horse is estranged from its innate nature, stoically hiding physical, emotional, and mental pain from us humans. These words describe a horse in a partial freeze or collapse state—able to appear as normal but not completely present and responsive. A horse or human who has adapted by withdrawing (a feature of immobilization) may display awkward and explosive bouts of energy when coming out from those withdrawn states. You may have heard of this if you haven't personally experienced it. The "dead broke" horse who suddenly twists and bucks and gallops off without any thought to what direction it's going or who is on its back—that's the awakening from dullness. It's scary for the horse and it's scary for us.

It's easy for our bodies to remember a past threat and re-experience it as a current threat. If we can avoid re-triggering overwhelm, we can come out of collapse or freeze instead of going back into that state. Our systems respond to threat without distinguishing between imagined threat, remembered threat, or actual threat. Our internal sensors develop the unconscious belief habit that coming out of collapse or freeze is life-threatening, so best to stay in the state where we know we will survive.

How can we avoid this overwhelm as we come out of either freeze or collapse into a more settled state? The company of a safe person—someone who can help regulate us while slowing the process—will help us stay connected with the present moment (*I am alive*) even as we have one foot in the memory of the past overwhelm (*I am about to die*).

This healing happens when we briefly experience a little bit of the big activation connected to the memory, then bring full attention to the present moment—with guidance from the safe person if needed—and take whatever time it takes for the natural discharge and settling and integration to happen. Remember the wave imagery? The wave of high sympathetic activation crests, then settles, and there's the pause, resting in the trough. My Somatic Experiencing® Practitioner was my safe person while a body memory surfaced. Her presence and skills allowed my previously buried sympathetic activation to surface in full force, then peak, then settle and start the integration of what had happened many years before.

I like the notion of middle-whelm, a tolerable state between overwhelm and underwhelm. Some know this as our "window of tolerance." When overwhelmed, we can't think clearly or act in accordance with the developed principles and mores of our rational brain. When underwhelmed, we don't have enough energy to take action; we're stuck in a semi-collapsed state that might be labeled depression or apathy. My goal is to have adequate access to a calmer, more settled state, and a handy road map for returning to this after those upsets in the normal course of life events.

We can *survive* facing all of our past pain at once, but if we want to heal, we allow only a little bit at a time. We let a little bit of pain surface and attend to that little bit. No hurry, lots of time to acquaint ourselves with the little bit. This allows for the settling and integration of the energy shift that occurs when the held energy of past overwhelm is discharged. And this permits the changed sense of self to emerge.

To help our horses come out of immobility or a high anxiety state, we need to be that attentive, safe presence for them. Charlie needed me to be calm—calm enough to perceive how much he wanted to be close to the group of horses, and to help him get there. Realizing I had not noticed Charlie's pleas prompted me to further develop my capacity to be calm. When we can calm ourselves, our horses have a chance to find calm as well.

As we wonder about our own autonomic nervous system states or those of a rider, a colleague, family member, or horse, let's consider that we all have parts. Many are survival parts organized for connection, play, sharing, and getting along in a way that is relaxed and brings the possibility of feeling a sense of safety while being close to others. Ideally our parts work well together, a collaborative team where each part has a voice and feels heard and valued by the other parts, and where all parts are welcome.

But the ideal is just that: an ideal that seldom matches reality, because getting along is complicated when the needs of some parts conflict with the needs of other parts. Despite wanting to be in harmony, we experience discord, discomfort, and dissonance between parts.

Binds arise when our parts have conflicting priorities and impulses, such as getting along in order to belong in a herd; running from danger; fighting a threat; and collapsing or freezing because nothing else promises survival. We never get to say, "Ah, this is how to respond to this situation." Our physiology responds without input from our reasoning mind, like Christy's fearful parts showing up in her body even though her getting-along parts were ready to trust us and enjoy the process of learning to ride.

Let's look at the survival parts of me as a therapeutic riding instructor. I am one member of a team when I'm teaching. Getting along with others, plus the people-pleasing factor, means the socially engaged part of my parasympathetic nervous system is active along with mild sympathetic arousal due to wanting to please others. Conflicting survival parts show up when I worry that a worried horse might cause harm to a rider. My attention narrows to the horse. As my vision becomes focused, I lose track of most everything else in the environment, including how the volunteers are faring with this worried horse and vulnerable rider. Another part of me notices that I'm not seeing the whole picture, and then becomes self-critical and freezes. Yet another part is confident it'll all work out and tries to reassure my worried part, urging me to carry on.

What about the parts of our horses? What are their survival parts? Same as ours, I suspect. Safely engaged parts: *I'm relaxing in the barn, standing quietly in cross ties, feeling fine as I'm being groomed by someone I like.* A muck fork falls to the floor. Sympathetic arousal parts: *What's that? Do I need to run for my life?* Stronger sympathetically activated parts: *I'm trapped by these cross ties but I'm in mortal danger and must run for my life.*

Survival parts are compelling. Horses don't convince themselves with reasons why it's safe to stand still. Like humans, they *will* just stand there when they have lost access to their fight and flight responses. Those dead-broke horses are the scariest to me, because when they reconnect with their thwarted fight and flight response? Look out!

Being able to shift states and have opportunities for engagement with others—and for fun, curiosity, a mix of novelty and routine, and space to move—are all part of a healthy autonomic nervous system. Collapse and freeze aren't necessarily problems. Being stuck in those states is the concern. Hence, knowing how to come out of immobilization and having the capacity to be with what lies beneath—that's the exit route from the deceptive quiet of shut down.

Meanwhile, I wonder. How can I lend a hand to those people

who are on a path of self-reflection, learning, and recovery from past overwhelm? How can I lend a hand to those who want a better relationship with themselves and their horses?

We begin to befriend the fear, anger, and disappointment that arise, to welcome the no as well as the yes. We stop fighting against what happens. We stop being critical of our responses. We start looking for opportunities to bring kindness to all parts of ourselves.

We tend to feel safe when our horse is doing what we want. We don't feel safe when our horse perceives danger then fast and furiously attends to its own survival. I want things to go well in therapy programs for all involved. I want horses and humans alike to be thriving, not just surviving. Which means we need to explore how to let our horses be fully themselves—curious and taking initiative—enough to balance out their hours of acting in compliance with our plans and needs. We do survive together, but can we thrive together?

Part Three:
Progress, Not Perfection

CHAPTER 8

Boundaries

Daring to set boundaries is about having the courage to love ourselves even when we risk disappointing others.
— Brené Brown

Repairing attachment and boundary ruptures helps increase our capacity for connection and closeness.
— Sarah Schlote

Don't Tell Me What to Do

"Rusty is just like me," I heard myself say, during one of the many conversations in my head in which I dissect events and emotions and attempt to make sense of my relationships. "He hates being told what to do." It fit when I heard it in my head, but then, thinking more about it, it didn't fit.

During that mental conversation, I was recalling participating in a five-day horsemanship clinic with Harry Whitney. I'd driven from Vermont to Tennessee in my older but trustworthy, maroon-colored GMC, with Rusty behind me in the bright red stock trailer.

During the clinic, I did my best to follow Harry's suggestions as I was riding. I may have been practicing gentling my hands on the reins, or being consistent when I asked for direction, or continuing to ask until Rusty responded, instead of giving up and asking for something else. Whatever it was, I had to settle into a meditative state of thought suspension in order to listen to Harry, do what

Harry suggested, and subdue my own feelings of confusion and conflict about not knowing everything already . . . all at the same time.

Rusty yawned and relaxed, starting to let down mentally and emotionally like I'd never felt him do before. He patiently waited for my next indication of a boundary, a *yes this* or a *no, not that*. It was sweet. Unspeakably sweet. Bring-tears-to-your-eyes sweet.

I scratched my head in wonder many times during that clinic. I have habitually offered my horses a lot of choice, and it baffled me to get this melting response from Rusty when I was—in my interpretation—giving him so few choices.

I did not follow up after the clinic with regular riding or with offering him as much direction and support as I did in that clinic. Mea culpa. But I kept thinking about his response. I started recognizing that it was *my* dislike of being told what to do that made it hard for me to be in the role of telling Rusty what to do.

But what if he really needed that from me? Could I let go of my own stuck place and give him what he needed? Could I do this without the prickly emotions that tended to surface when I was being told what to do and had some other superb ideas about what I should be doing? I was feeling defensive but didn't want to respond that way.

Rusty was not the only one who got the brunt of my emotional upsets. The people in my life have as well. The progress I'm making—fewer upsets spilling onto loved ones—is about all I can ask for.

That Far Away

Emily was brought by her mother to the therapeutic riding program, where she participated each week in the equine-assisted mental health program. She was a shy, well-mannered, slightly-built eight-year-old when we met, and after a year she started to talk with me in full sentences and make eye contact. She'd always been capable of talking, but her social withdrawal dominated, and her learned submissiveness eclipsed any budding assertiveness she might have felt. I asked a lot of questions. She answered a few of those questions with averted eyes, slumped posture, and either a mumbled yes, or silence. I guessed her silence meant either no or, "I don't want to even think about that question." The main times she looked up, lit up, and expressed enthusiasm were when I asked, "Would you like to head out for some horse time now?" Our expressive arts and chatting time shifted to her getting on a horse and riding.

Emily loved horseback riding. She had already learned basic skills thanks to lessons at another facility. Although she had learned a more rigid, rule-bound way of riding and relating with horses than I liked, she had natural balance and a big heart. She also had a very broken heart. That brokenness left her in a bind about directing the horse. If I could give her words, she would be saying to the horse, "I want to go there. You're not going there. What am I doing wrong? Why aren't you listening to me? I give up . . ."—with six seconds between "I want" and "I give up." She was a very sad young girl, already living in an unfulfilled state of wanting, with no belief that she could have what she wanted. No confidence. Persistence had been replaced long ago by her readiness to give up and sink into herself. Learned helplessness. A state of partial immobilization.

I designed Emily's riding time based on simple patterns, arranging barrels and colored cones in the arena so she could make detailed decisions about which barrels she would circle and which cones she would ride to. My unspoken intention was that she enjoy being in charge of what she was doing, and, I hoped, gain confidence in her ability to make good decisions based on what she wanted.

To support Emily's success without intruding, I hung back while she rode, standing near her mother at ringside. Her mother was educated, accomplished, anxious, and overwhelmed with work and parenting. She was used to giving directions and was bothered that her older children were rebelling against her authority and fighting with each other. She had welcomed Emily's quiet moods, not seeing beyond the pleasant and compliant to the withdrawn and miserable. At first, depression and withdrawal had led Emily to refuse to join family activities. Then she developed clearer ways of saying no. Eventually she said no to coming to riding time with me, after she learned from a school friend that where she was riding was a therapeutic riding program, not a normal lesson barn. She balked.

Before she balked, we had a lesson I'll always remember. Emily put into words some agitation about her mother while coloring a picture of a smiling horse standing in a green field with colorful flowers and a cloudless blue sky. All things in the picture were peaceful, in contrast to the angry disempowered parts of her that were starting to feel safe to show up. I had the idea to explore boundaries experientially with her and her mother right there and then. We left the office and walked to where her mother was busy on her phone.

"Emily, would you like to play around with how much distance you might like from your mother?"

"Yes," she affirmed, nodding her head.

I turned to her mother. "You willing to try this?"

"Yes," she said, as desperate as ever to do whatever she could to help her daughter. She was becoming aware of Emily's moods and was increasingly worried about their relationship and about how often Emily had been saying no to family and school activities.

"Emily, if you can, would you tell your mom where to stand? She's willing to move to where you'd like her to be here at the farm. We'll play around with where's the best place that helps you feel good about the distance between you and your mom."

Emily was brave that day. Over the next five minutes, she directed her mother to the far side of the parking area, far enough away that we had to raise our voices to be heard. I noticed Emily was starting to relax—her shoulders dropped, her voice got fuller, her eyes softened and she started to look around. In this moment, her mother was the right amount of far enough away.

Meanwhile, off in the distance, I could see her mother's torso collapse. Her body posture told a story of feeling hurt, and the shock and disbelief about her daughter's need for that much distance.

I paused to honor Emily's choices and her annoyance that her mother was upset by her need for this distance, then gestured to the volunteer who was waiting with Emily's horse who was groomed, tacked, and ready to be mounted. I told her mother I'd support her in a moment after supervising Emily as she mounted, adjusted stirrups, and made a riding plan. Then I turned my attention to her distraught mother.

The good news is we had been building a relationship during the previous year, and she had been seeing her own therapist for longer than that. She had some knowledge about trauma and had started healing from her own family wounding. We stood near the rail of the riding arena, some of our attention on Emily's riding patterns, some of our attention on settling the big waves of activation that she had experienced. She could identify some of her triggers, but she had some difficulty separating her historical triggers and unmet needs left over from her own childhood, from the wounded feelings that surfaced as her daughter asserted herself that day.

This Much Space

Every therapeutic riding program needs a good pony. Ideally, this good pony is a middle-aged gelding with lots of training and experience and is comfortable being ridden by a variety of riders—both leadline riders and independent riders—and moving into all the crazy adventures a child could think of. A good pony enjoys the company of humans, whether for grooming, standing around getting scratched, or being led in lessons. A good pony can safely carry smaller riders as well as riders who need lots of help from sidewalkers. A good pony is the right size for limiting strain on the sidewalkers who are actively holding balance for the hippotherapy riders. These riders come for equine-assisted physical therapy, occupational therapy, or speech and language therapy because they would benefit from the walking rhythm of the horse even if they need hands-on support to keep them there. Some of these riders are carried to the horse, placed on the horse, and held on the horse until they are lifted off the horse and returned to their wheelchairs or parents' arms.

Theo was our hope for fulfilling the Good Pony role. He was the right size. He had tons of training and tons of experience. Much to our chagrin, he wasn't fond of people walking close to him, nor of carrying an imbalanced rider. Even being led wasn't his cup of tea. He knew how to be ridden by an independent rider and he knew how to walk, trot, canter, gallop, jump, and back up. All these activities were within his comfort zone when he was being guided by a skilled rider on his back. All this other stuff that happens in a therapeutic riding lesson? No thanks.

He tried. He tried really hard. When his distress became obvious and his behaviors were scaring staff and volunteers, I was asked to help.

I loved learning about Theo and what made sense to him. I worked primarily from the ground with leading and lunging activities, although I rode him once to experience how he responded to the common cues used when riding. He and I got along well after I took the time to earn his trust. He needed to trust me to make requests that he could understand and to consider his responses. Often this meant asking slowly and waiting patiently for his answer, moving through molasses rather than rafting through whitewater. Once he understood, then faster was fine.

My goal was to help him feel okay when people directed him while standing near his head and leading him, or walking close to his sides and back legs. That is where most of the problems appeared—ears back, turning to nip his leader. Lifting a hind leg as a message to back off, following his initial and unnoticed requests for more space around his barrel and hind end. He was uncomfortable with people walking close to him and didn't particularly like horses or humans near him at all unless it was part of a grooming, tacking, or riding activity.

I had fun helping him gain some comfort with these things. I enjoyed going slowly, so slowly that Theo had time to think about what I was asking of him. So slowly that I could see his mind working before he responded to my requests. So much of this was around boundaries. Those almost nonexistent boundaries we relied on in our therapeutic riding lessons—the ones that allowed us to be in close proximity all the time—were a foreign language to him. *Why are these people so close to me?* And what he didn't understand, he wanted nothing to do with. He was threatened by new things. After all, he was a middle-aged, well-trained equine. He knew what he knew, and didn't wake up each day with a strong yearning to learn new things. Not Theo. So how to work with a solidly-trained horse who had no interest in learning and adjusting to new conditions?

I started with what he knew, and let him know in our nonverbal horsey/human ways that I got it, I understood his preferences and would honor them. I vowed to listen to his preferences when we were together, even though I wouldn't be able to protect him from being asked by others to do some things he did not understand or want to do.

My challenge was and continues to be this: How can I help a horse adjust to other people? I can help them adjust to what I want. I do that in little steps, building from one tolerable adjustment or learning event to the next, to the next such as being okay with someone walking along near his barrel. I led him and I lunged him, two things he understood pretty well. Slowly I moved my position so I was leading him from his shoulder, and eventually from his side and then from near his hip. This was like lunging, but being really close. There was the possibility that he could shift from "I know how to lunge" to "Oh, hey, this is lunging too, but a little different."

My practice of checking in with his comfort and frame of mind is what I find hard to teach others. And that's the key to gaining and keeping a horse's trust and attention and involvement. When Theo looked to me for confirmation that he was doing what was asked—because once again he was confused by a slightly different way of being asked—I was there nonverbally through eye contact and breathing and nodding my head, letting him know, "Yup, this is what your rider or leader is asking. Perfect, Theo. You got this." This conversation can occur silently across the ring. We developed a connection that included checking in with each other. Horses need connection and support, not just direction now and then. Some horses need it more than others. Theo preferred to be connected and guided and affirmed. When not, he was on his own in his little horsey mind, fending for himself because he didn't have a sense that someone was present and attentive, and helping him navigate this confusing world of humans.

I understand frustration about communication. I understand how scary it is to try to do what's expected while having no idea what's expected. Like when I don't know if I'm meant to reach up with my left arm, or out, or down. I've been taking yoga classes online during this pandemic. I love what I gain from the classes. The teacher is extremely skilled and has a toolbox of yoga postures from decades of teaching. In person, she could walk over and guide my position for new learning, new neural pathways, new details in my brain's body map, in my capacity to move and stretch the ways we're designed to.

But it all falls apart when I don't understand what I'm meant to be doing. I fall apart when I'm partially understanding directions. Not only am I angry because I'm confused, but I'm disappointed because I feel so desperate at times for help to have a better-functioning body, more aliveness, less constriction, less pain and fear. And I suppose part of this stems from the fact that we're on Zoom. I can see her and hear her, but all the students are muted as she talks us through the class. So there is no way I can communicate my need to her, no way I can send a signal cry to her that I am in confusion and that confusion is building to distress.

That night technology saved me. I'd been lying there, tears streaming down my cheeks, feeling lost and alone and unsure what to do. Wi-Fi failed, and I lost connection with the Zoom class.

I was flooded with relief. My struggle to understand what I was supposed to be doing came to an end.

I can imagine what Theo felt like when he couldn't make sense of our human communication. He was a kind, gentle horse, and kind, gentle horses want to get along. He wanted to get along with us humans because it feels good to work as a team. That pleasant sense of cooperation exists in peaceful herd environments. But when messages don't make sense, and some of the lesson team "herd" are careless with words or handling—when the humans become fearful and unaware of their own fear—it's rough for a horse like Theo.

I just want to get along, too, and I want to learn. I wanted to practice the yoga as intended, for the best possible outcome. I wanted my teacher to be successful, and I wanted to feel safe with her—but in those moments, I did not. I couldn't follow what she was saying. I was distressed and had no way to tell her. Theo, on the other hand, had ways to tell us we were not communicating successfully. He could pin his ears; he could brace against any request that confused him; he could kick out if his capacity for feeling pressured—or for trying something that didn't make sense to him—fell short of his ability to remain tolerant.

Boundaries

Skin is our most obvious boundary. It contains us and protects us, defining the line between what's my body and what's not my body, what's within skin and outside of skin.

Skin is where we sense touch, pleasant or otherwise. Touch intrusions—when we lose choice about being touched—are common, such as when a stranger touches a pregnant woman's belly or a family member hugs a child without checking for permission. Even when the doctor whose job includes touching us, presses through skin to palpate organs.

Like Theo, we have space boundaries, too. Some describe these as bubbles whose walls ideally are permeable and adjustable so that we can let in some and keep out some. Space intrusions are as real as skin contact intrusions. Neuroception (our automatic internal scanning of people, places, and things) tells us if we are safe or not when someone is near—whether they are touching us or not.

Most of us override the directives from our senses, ignoring information about what's the right space between I and Thou. Imagine you're about to get a tetanus shot from your trusted doctor. You know you want it in order to prevent an excruciating death from tetany, a death which cannot be prevented once symptoms occur. You've made a clear choice in favor of getting this shot. You like your doctor. For years she has been kind and attentive and helpful, even has a sense of humor. But your body says, "To hell with this! I don't care how kind she's been, she's about to stab me with a sharp metal object that will break my skin and force some foreign substance into my body! Let's get out of here, now!" The body is saying "No, no, no!" even while the mind is saying, "Yes, please."

Horses don't have the human ability to inhibit large surges of fear in order to adhere to what's expected of them. Running when frightened is the norm for horses. Standing still when scared is what we do when we prioritize keeping someone else relatively calm for our own sense of safety—rather than following our own urges to move away from perceived danger. Then there's Rusty. Just by owning him, I was intruding on his freedom. But he needed more boundary-setting from me—through the reins, for example—in order to feel connected with me and understand my guidance.

We all override personal space boundaries. Imagine being at a social gathering and someone attractive walks toward you, showing interest in engaging with you. As they approach, you get a whiff of their cologne, and you're holding your breath to avoid smelling it. One part of you is saying, "I want to get to know this person," and another part is saying, "I'll die if I can't get away." A simple conflict between these opposing tendencies.

These moments of overriding our own boundaries leave us with unexpressed conflicts about proximity. Emily had been living with suppressed longings. She was a child, reliant on her family, yet closeness had become an obligation. That started to change when she created distance from her mother. Hidden wants wait for an opportunity to find release through action. We humans may be able to bury these wants from our awareness, but our horses cannot. Our horses want congruency between impulse and action. They want clear boundaries with us, and consistent boundaries. It's key to their feeling safe within their herd. Even when it's a very subtle communication about space: a look, an ear movement, a shift of weight. *This is my space. I will share this space. I will not share this space.*

I was raised to comply, to say yes to requests, and to allow parents, teachers, and medical professionals to come close, even touch me. Missing in my upbringing was encouragement to say no or "Stay away!" As an adult, my discomfort with stating these boundaries weakened my budding resolve to speak up about what I need. When I feel supported for setting boundaries, my inner vulnerable parts are more likely to show up, dance with me, scream with me, throw punches with me, step closer for hugs with me.

With boundary intrusions also occurring on the level of belief systems, social group norms, and prescribed behaviors, there's a fine line between too little and too much input from outside ourselves. As a child in my family and in school, my success relied on obedience. Other people told me what to do, what to think, how to stand, when to move, who could be my friend. Without some adherence to social norms, I would have been too wild, too threatening, too little understood. That would have conflicted with my desire to fit in and be part of my human herd.

Boundaries are meant to be determined by the individual, based on ever-fluctuating needs for closeness and distance. This is true for horses as well as humans. Rusty wanted more contact with me. Emily and Theo wanted more distance.

If I say, "Back off!" as someone approaches, I might offend. Like Emily, I can feel reluctant to express my need for distance. I prefer when others do not take it personally and do not get upset, and I certainly prefer it if they don't attack me for setting the boundaries I need in that moment. To set a boundary is an act of self-care. Although the criteria for feeling safe will change, the criteria are real, reflecting what is happening in the moment. To support others to set boundaries is a way to honor them. The biggest challenge seems to be honoring my own boundaries while honoring someone else's.

Boundary ruptures in relationships are common, seldom repaired, and often not even noticed. The not-noticing happens with humans, but not so much with horses.

My mare Kacee was the teacher of acceptable horse behavior in my herd. I observed her setting boundaries day after day with Rusty. Twice, Kacee intervened to assist me because of my inadequate boundaries with Rusty. She came between us and bit him hard on the withers when he was pushing into my space and I was unable to stop him. Rusty was isolated in early life from other horses who would have taught him what the social expectations were. He came to me as a yearling without much understanding of yielding—of, "Okay, you want some space, I'll step away." I had my own history of space intrusions and had not yet learned that I could set boundaries and survive. My boundary setting was tangled with terror and rage, with feeling threatened and furious. Kacee simply did her horsey thing to stop him, and provide safety for me, as part of her herd. Her message was something along the lines of, "If you can't play nice, Rusty, go away. Come back when you can." I appreciated what Kacee did to keep me safe, but it is our job to determine our own boundaries and then help the horse or the spouse or the friend understand and respect them.

Even though the importance of boundaries seems obvious among horses, we humans are just as aware as they are of the space between ourselves and others, even if unconsciously. Horses check boundaries within their herd again and again. I suspect boundaries are just as critical to us, but we are often in conflict, with our yearning for closeness overriding any need for distance.

Those of us who teach others about horses—whether through groundwork or through riding activities—need to be mindful of our own boundaries with the students, the lesson volunteers, and the horses. My boundary expectations may differ from theirs. Volunteers and riders might have more casual conversations when I'm not present, especially if they know each other from the community, not just from the riding lessons.

When I'm responsible for student safety—in an emergency dismount situation for example—I may step in and touch the student without getting consent first, because there just may not be time for consent in a crisis.

What can I do to have better boundaries with my students, my friends, my family members, my pets? How do I know if my boundaries are too few, too weak, too many, too rigid, or just right? Each horse, like each of us humans, will have a changing mix of needs for space, for closeness, and for structure, as well as for guidance, direction, containment, and help to focus. It's all about feeling safe and being aware.

Most of us mingle regularly with other people and animals. How do we separate ourselves from the emotional or energetic states of others? Think about having an anxious parent leaning on the rail of the arena fence, calling out directions to the child who is a student in the lesson. Hands on the rail, face looking worried, voice high-pitched and fast. How do we *not* get involved with that energy state? How do we *not* get involved with the energy of a worried horse? Or with that of a volunteer who's trying to keep a rider safe but feels anxious because the horse is too big, or the horse is too fast, or the horse just lifted a hind leg as if to kick?

CHAPTER 9

Body Language

You know, the most important thing in communication is to hear what isn't being said. — PETER DRUCKER

My Teacher

MY TEACHER, RUSTY. The one who prompts me to think, and think, and think some more. About horses. What is a horse, what matters to a horse, how does a horse understand? What does a person do to confuse a horse, to upset a horse? To calm a horse, direct a horse, gain a horse's trust? To elicit a horse's willingness to be together?

I blame myself, and take credit, for all Rusty has become over the decades. Our long, complicated relationship started when he was six months old. Things have changed. I understand body language better. I listen better to him. He responds with more readiness than before, with more attention and relaxation in my presence. I must be offering him something he understands and likes.

I've been committed to keeping his integrity as a horse intact. He is comfortable expressing his opinions. I'm not always at ease with his opinions because at times they have come as ears pinned, or with a kick. But I am determined to accept that he needs to express himself, and to be kind and skillful asking him to change his mind when I've wanted or needed that, whether I'm on the ground with him haltered, or mounted and riding. If he's doing his own thing in the herd, he's free to act however he likes. I consider it my responsibility to engage his consent and curiosity as much as possible in order to do the things I hope we will do together. Even when I'm scared.

A friend once told me, "Rusty is a horse that will make a horseman out of you." It was years before I started to understand what she meant. I'd fallen in love with a weanling stuck in a stall—this wicked-cute fellow, spirited and very willing to try to get along with me. That was our beginning. Many years later, I came to a new place regarding relationships, empathy, and understanding horses. I started riding him as if it were our first few rides, with careful attention to his emotions and helping him feel good about what I was asking of him.

I wanted to regain that original unassuming connection between us that I recalled from our early rides. He'd been confused by me since then—I'd asked for too much, too soon, too quickly. My body language sent mixed messages. I began making efforts to be clear and patient with him, instead of getting irked thinking that he was refusing to do what I asked. I wanted to foster his curiosity about what I was asking. I wanted to avoid repeating those mired, heavy, conflicted experiences where he wanted to be doing one thing, and I wanted to be doing another thing, and *yuck*. It felt awful to both of us.

Contact with fellow travelers on the trail of good horsemanship helped me focus on learning to offer something better to horses. Rusty's changes were a tribute to the kind attention and interventions of my more-knowledgeable friends and mentors. My adaptation of the saying, "It takes a community to raise a child," is this: "It takes a community to develop a good horseperson." Notice I said horse *person*. I needed the help, not Rusty.

My community includes people and horses. I am much closer to my ideal than ever before—the ideal of learning directly through relating with horses. This is progress beyond learning from the interpretations of other horse people, my translators as I was learning to understand and feel the horse's communication.

"Horse" is a language that exists within a complex of equine social norms, more novel to me than those I've encountered in diverse human communities.

I know how to study sounds and develop a new way of speaking words and concepts in order to communicate using a new spoken language. I enjoyed studying French, Italian, and Mandarin in school. Applying my skills with spoken language is meaningless with horses. Their language is without words. Their speech is formed by the observable body and the invisible energy fields. I don't always understand their language, while they often understand my unspoken meaning before I do.

Horses are my teachers whenever I relinquish any notion that they are my students. These horses are my community, where I get a sense of belonging.

Adjusting Plans

Another experiment was brewing. I was all set to ride to a local farm stand, about three miles down one of the gravelly dirt roads that were abundant in the hilly rural area of New Hampshire where I was living. It would be a ride with a purpose, a shopping trip on horseback. I wanted to find a reason for horse time other than the arena riding I did to improve my skills or train the horses.

I had ridden my mare Kacee the day before, and hadn't ridden Rusty much at all, so I figured I'd ride Soli, my dear been-there-done-that Haflinger.

But Soli was lame—weight-bearing, but gimpy. I guessed he'd had an unplanned slide in the rain-soaked fields. I brought him in, checked him over, groomed him, and turned him out in the paddock behind the barn.

I stood wondering what to do as my disappointment dissipated. My young chestnut mare Riza came to mind. I could spend time with her. She was just starting to learn about wearing a saddle. I had saddled her a few times and she had been a little concerned about the saddle pad—eyes widening, a hitch in her breath—but had allowed me to set it on her back.

One way that horses learn is by social modeling, by watching what other horses do. I had read this and then experienced it vividly when I taught my horses to stand with their front feet on a low wooden platform (built to withstand the weight of a horse). It took some time for the first horse to figure out what I wanted, then each of the others who had been grazing close enough to watch, stepped up on it the first or second time I asked them to.

So when Riza showed some hesitancy about the saddle pad, I turned to Kacee, who was dozing nearby, and rubbed it on her while Riza watched, then brought it back to Riza. I repeated this until Riza was fine with my bringing it toward her. Next, I set it on her back and then took it off from each side before I left it there and added the saddle. Riza was calm—head low, eyes soft, breath slow and steady.

I thought she was ready to experience more new stimuli, so I gathered her halter and lead rope, some rhythm bells (a necklace with beads and small bells that can calm a horse, even improve its cadence) to drape around her neck, and some reflective ankle cuffs with Velcro closure, and we headed for the round pen.

I asked her to walk and trot in both directions wearing the saddle before I put the cuffs on her front ankles and asked her to walk and trot in both directions again. The cuffs were to help her accept things around her ankles. One day we might run into some fallen fencing on a trail ride, and if she was okay with cuffs on her ankles, she might be okay with fencing on her ankles. Exposing her to wearing cuffs was the first of many things I could do to help her stay calm, should that happen.

I moved the ankle cuffs to her hind ankles and again asked her to walk and trot in both directions. I removed the cuffs and put the rhythm bells around her neck. Walk and trot both directions. I removed the bells and hung her halter over the saddle horn. Walk and trot both directions.

Riza was undisturbed. This filly had a gentle nature and was moderately ready to yield within her herd. To me, this meant she would be more likely to try my suggestions rather than resist them. She had had little handling, most of which had been simple and understandable for her—stand for hoof trimming, stand for grooming, follow whoever carries the lead rope. Because she didn't need help unlearning fear-induced protective responses, we could simply proceed without fanfare, if I behaved myself. I am certain that my efforts to expose her in little increments were part of why this all went so well.

Overwhelm doesn't just come when a deer comes scooting across the trail. It comes when we ask a horse to learn too much, too fast. Because I was seldom in a hurry then, it was easy to proceed slowly through the lessons I wanted to introduce to this sweet horse.

I suppose it helped that during that time I'd been teaching more therapeutic riding lessons. And there, I was continuously seeking to introduce ideas in ways that my students had the best chance of understanding. For some, that meant I might use two to three words and model an action—and wait. For others, it meant I gently held their hands and did the action with them, time after time after time. At some point it would click and they could do what I asked without my hands to help.

I knew a little about patience. Although that frame of mind was not always accessible to me, I strove to have it be regular in my life. Patience suits the horses, whom I sometimes think of as three- or four-year-old children. Would we start yelling and slapping a three-year-old who didn't understand what we wanted? I hope not. (Though having worked in child protective services early in my social work career, I know that some children do indeed get hurt due to the misunderstandings and frustrations of their caregivers. I am not naive about that.)

As long as I brought my best to the barn and was present and focused on helping Riza learn what humans might want from her, at a pace that made sense to her, I had a good chance of ending up with a fun horse to ride. "Fun" to me meant I would be on a horse who understood what I wanted us to do, felt good about my requests, and was somewhere between willing and eager to do things with me.

Both Mark Rashid and Harry Whitney spoke of this sense of doing things together. This was not about me learning the nicest way to make my horse do something, even though that felt better than using less nice ways to make a horse do things. Instead, I was practicing thinking, "Let's do this together. If you aren't able or willing to do this with me right now, what can I do so you might change your mind? Can I help you feel that connecting with me is a good idea?"

I mention this because when I was with Riza and we did all that walk-and-trot-both-directions, it wasn't always that smooth. She had her mild ways of leaving me mentally: heading to sniff a pile of manure, slowing near where the other horses were hanging out outside the round pen, changing direction when I hadn't asked for that. But she was easy to redirect. I'd kept things as clear and simple as I knew how. I was thankful for this opportunity to experiment with a young horse, drawing on the best of what I'd learned.

I got along fabulously with my other horses when I treated them like I was treating Riza. Each encounter was fresh. With each activity, I was asking, "How well do you know how to do this? Any confusion? OK, let's review this before we proceed."

Conflict in Action

I'd recently relocated from New Hampshire to Maine, and was finding my way in a new home, a new community, and a new job. I was pleased to be asked to develop a program that brought together my clinical social work and therapeutic riding instructor professions. This was designed for people who had difficulties engaging and functioning in life.

It lit me up to be asked, though it also brought anxiety. I'd been more a follower of others and not much of a leader, although I'd done my share of proselytizing over the years. Me, the Queen-Know-It-All, intent on sharing it all.

Experiential education was a key element of this program. I've loved learning by doing activities rather than from reading books or listening to lectures. My program allowed me to set up learning opportunities, guide self-reflection, and support whatever joys and challenges would be ready to surface and be experienced by the participants. I wove expressive arts and horse activities into an hour-long weekly plan. We would spend the first half hour talking and drawing in a barn office setting, and the second half hour with a horse and the necessary volunteers.

A tall, disheveled-looking young adult named Teresa was my first student in this program. She came somewhat for herself and somewhat because her mother wanted her to change. Teresa's curiosity about horses helped. She brought a bit more interest than fear of them to our time together.

In most areas of her life, Teresa had little interest and lots of hesitation. She had slowly constricted to the point of living with her mother again after failing at living on her own, failing at attending college, failing at having an intimate relationship. Her life seemed to be defined by her failures.

The most obvious expression of her distress was her walking away from her goals, counter to her intended direction. She was uncertain about most everything, painfully disconnected from any self-confidence, and these traits showed up as she actually moved from one place to the next. She would physically face her destination while actively retreating. It was only with concerted effort that she moved from the car to the office. Her body said, "Stand still," while her mind pushed her to start walking. It was with similar effort that she moved from the office to the riding ring where a therapy horse waited for her—one she would interact with, mount, and ride.

She stuttered with words, and she stuttered with movement—as though she was acting out a major conflict between internal parts that said, "Yes, let's do this!" and parts that said, "Nope, no way."

I wish I'd known more when I met with her. I hadn't yet had the training in somatic trauma resolution that has changed my life and my professional practice. I can envision more interventions and psychoeducation I would have offered her. I would have encouraged her to explore walking with me by her side, alternating with backward steps and forward steps, letting her whole being experience support as she attended to what it was like to go each direction. We'd add stepping sideways and stepping in arcs and diagonals, with many pauses between transitions.

The interventions I did offer then were listening without judgment and helping her ride. I knew the walking movement of the horse would help her body remember how to ambulate in a forward direction. And indeed, when she dismounted at the end of each riding time, her first steps were graceful, and forward.

Body Language

Body language reveals the stories that words can't tell. It is our universal language, and our first language. All bodies speak through eyes, breath, posture, stillness, and movement. Spoken language—overvalued in our culture—will always be our second language.

Although we're conditioned to pay attention to words, we are neurologically wired to notice what's not said in words, what the bodies are saying. Neuroception is the internal sense that registers our responses to people, places, and things as *I'm safe* or *I'm not safe*. But we often ignore the messages from our senses, overriding them to avoid overwhelm. To get through the day, I don't want *all* the truth *all* the time. I need breaks from reality. For example, I could never drive on a highway at sixty miles per hour without a significant amount of denial. Sensory override will shield me from feeling vulnerable hurtling through space close to other objects doing the same.

Noticing the body language of others can be like watching the beacon from a lighthouse on a foggy night. The light—the body's message—radiates outward in all directions. The light is shining but muted by the fog, altering how the light is perceived. Our beliefs and our trained social behaviors are the fog that distorts the message from the lighthouse.

Sometimes our word stories contradict our body stories. Think of someone saying "I'm fine" even though you observe a grimace, slumped posture, or an unusual limp. With humans, these mixed messages are the norm. Our unconscious, unresolved troubles from the past live in our here-and-now bodies, as with Teresa. She thought she wanted to walk forward to the riding ring, but her steps took her backward, away from her intended destination.

With non-verbal species like horses, there are no mixed messages. Congruence between the messages expressed through observable behaviors and the meaning of those messages is guaranteed. Think of the inexperienced mare who stands stock still, head high, eyes wide when she's first being handled. She is not moving, but her readiness to explode is tangible. We may miss the degree of sympathetic activation under the stillness, but it's there.

I'm puzzled by how hard it is to write about body language even though I spend much of my time in silence. I live and breathe body language in my daily contact with our animals, and in my professional life as a Somatic Experiencing® Practitioner. Listening for the unspoken messages and bringing attention to them is how I can help people resolve traumatic experiences from their preverbal times. I'm listening to the unspoken messages even with my human family and friends.

Listening and responding to the littlest messages from Riza is what helped us progress to her feeling okay wearing a saddle. In Somatic Experiencing®, this practice is called titration: exposing someone to small enough changes that the newness can be understood and integrated. This way communication can be effective.

With Rusty, I might have more easily responded to his emotions and confusion if he had said things like, "I'm scared when I'm away from my horse friends," or, "I don't know what you want when you start walking away from me, then pull on the lead rope." But he couldn't speak in my language, and I often failed to know what he needed from me. I still have only the signals from his facial expressions, breathing patterns, muscle tightness or flaccidity, and efforts to move with me—or away from me due to the discomfort my normal human ignorance has caused him.

Many of us prioritize learning to read body language because we want to communicate better with our animal friends. Noticing the details of body language is a start. Guessing at meaning comes next. Accurate interpretation comes last.

If body language is our most primal form of communication, how can we get better at understanding what we ourselves are expressing? Video recording is a great feedback tool for enhancing body awareness (although I've not often been eager for that degree of precise feedback). When riding in an indoor arena with a wall of mirrors, I have seen for myself the mismatches between what I thought I was doing and what I was actually doing. I suspect other riders have similar memories from lessons—like when I thought my leg was in the position the instructor directed, but then I saw in the mirror that my leg was somewhere else in space.

Slowing down while introducing one new stimulus at a time allows me to see how the horse responds to that and only that. If I present my ideas with body language, using consistent cues that are meant to initiate an activity, how do I know if my horse understands my cues? Am I paying attention to how my horse responds when I stand this way or move that way, when I'm looking here or facing in that direction?

I'm driven to get better at communicating with horses. I want to be clear and avoid confusing my horse. I also want to be able to calm myself. Faced with a scared horse's body language, I will probably feel threatened, and my protective responses will come alive. These will distort my thoughts about what the horse is actually trying to tell me. I need to know both my own autonomic nervous system state and my horse's. Am I calm? Angry? Excited? Worried? Sad? Is my horse calm? Angry? Excited? Worried? Sad?

When I have strong emotions—other than gratitude and delight—I've learned to step away from my horse until I've settled. My calm, attentive presence is the foundation for an effective conversation in body language.

CHAPTER 10

Communication

What if a horse's anxiety isn't a fault but instead an invitation to a conversation?
— Anna Blake

And the deepest level of communication is not communication, but communion. It is wordless. It is beyond words, and it is beyond speech, and it is beyond concept.
— Thomas Merton

Trailer Terror

Lizzy—a neighbor I left behind when I moved from Maine—was struggling and sent me an email asking for help with Baxter, her new horse. She wanted to go riding with friends, and that meant trailering to the nearby state park with its abundance of dirt roads suitable for horseback riding. But Baxter was saying, "No, I'm not going into a trailer again. Once was enough." We followed up with a phone call that evening.

Baxter's former owner had bullied him into the trailer, determined to complete the sales agreement by delivering Baxter to Lizzy. Lizzy hadn't seen this, but she heard his former owner bragging about overpowering Baxter to get him into the trailer. As I listened to Lizzy, my stomach tightened. I pictured Baxter more scared of the human forcing him than of the trailer. The trailer became the safer of two evils.

Despite knowing Baxter's trauma history, Lizzy got progressively upset as she told me about his refusals. "He's so stubborn!" I could hear her frustration at his not getting into the trailer. "He's so effing clever." I could hear her exasperation at his ability to move away from the trailer faster than she could stop him. "He's a trouble-maker!" I could sense her tight jaw as she related his latest gyrations to avoid the trailer. Her disappointment was huge. It was affecting how she spoke about him, and it would affect how she communicated to him.

I took a deep breath and then exhaled slowly, hoping to release my own frustration at hearing her complaints. I've been impatient with horses, and with horse owners, and felt ashamed afterwards. I wanted to remain calm and supportive of Lizzy. I figured she needed that from me more than anything else.

"He's not stubborn, Lizzy. He's looking after his survival. Please, nothing more than that. Let's figure out how you can help him feel like the trailer is not going to kill him." I paused. "First, we want to get him comfortable even thinking about it."

That is what I wanted her to understand. Helping Baxter would come in several steps, and they all involved clear communication. Perhaps if I kindled some hope for success, Lizzy could shift her emotional state. First, we wanted Baxter simply to think about the trailer without panicking. That meant no pressure to go into the trailer. No new worry added to what he already experienced near the trailer. To Baxter, the trailer was a dangerous trap. My goal was to help Lizzy help her horse get ready to step into the trailer, even if we had no control over how long that would take.

I did my best to talk her through how to help Baxter. "If he can think about the trailer without getting upset from 100 yards away, then start there."

"That far away?"

"Yes. Really. No closer until he's okay that far away."

"You're saying watch for him to start getting that scared look, and don't bring him any closer?" I could hear Lizzy sigh before she spoke again. "I'm not sure he'll ever go into the trailer."

"Well, we both know he has good reason not to. Yeah, it's harder because he has to unlearn from his scary experience, but you *can* help him."

"I sure hope so."

"Like I said, first you're looking for him to feel okay just looking at the trailer from as far away as he needs. Once he feels okay looking from there, *then* it's okay for you to ask him to take a step closer to the trailer. And that's all you'll ask that day." I heard Lizzy sigh again as she took this in. I interpreted her sigh to mean she understood and was ready to offer Baxter all the patience she could muster.

I suggested she repeat this for several days and see how far from the trailer Baxter would need to be in order to feel okay looking at the trailer. I reminded her to keep breathing herself, and to notice Baxter's breathing, his stance, looking for information about how relaxed he was. His body language would communicate his level of activation.

"When he looks at the trailer with both eyes and both ears, you'll know he's more curious than scared and trying to get away from it. So, when you see his eyes and ears showing interest in the trailer, lead him away so he can have a break from the pressure he's been feeling being that close to the trailer."

We talked about what she could do to offer him a release, like leading him further away from the trailer. "Your release is meant to tell him you understand how terrifying the trailer was, right? *It was scary!* And the people who forced him into the trailer, they added fear and worry to his already fearful and worried state of mind." I paused to make sure Lizzy was following my train of thought.

"Oh, yeah," she said slowly.

"And you're going to help him feel okay." I paused again, wanting her to believe my affirmation. "When he pauses to consider the trailer, that's all you'll ask. And you'll prove that by taking him away from the scary trailer and letting him settle. Because as far as he's concerned, he just survived thinking about the trailer. Thinking about it did not kill him. This is a big deal."

Lizzy texted me the next day. She had led Baxter to where he looked at the trailer and gave a big sigh, lowering his head and blinking his eyes a few times. Visible information—communication through behaviors that Lizzy saw and understood. Lizzy had stayed calm and offered Baxter all the time and good feelings she could, so he could feel safe enough to stop worrying. When he could let down his guard is when he became open to trying something different. Baxter needed to find that feeling place on his own, but Lizzy needed to set up the conditions. There was no way to force him to feel that.

Lizzy was developing her relationship skills through thoughtful, two-way communication with Baxter, being sensitive to his feelings as she was asking him to follow her direction. She continued to text me about their changes over the next few weeks. I could tell she was keeping her promise to herself and to Baxter. She used her patience and her ability to calm herself. This set the tone for her communications to be heard by Baxter. She relied on realistic plans instead of her muscles and her inclination to fight with and overpower Baxter—a battle of strength she would never win. She delayed going for those trail rides. She chose to gain Baxter's confidence and trust first.

That is what gave Baxter a sense of having a say in the matter. If we want a horse with a cooperative attitude and thinking mind—one who will give us his best from his heart, not from a fearful, resigned, resentful place—we need to take the time to refine our skills of observing with all of our senses, as well as to develop new handling habits. It feels better to both horse and human when we're cooperating instead of pushing and resisting or resigning.

I'm not sure how many of us fully understand how our emotional tone affects the results we're getting with our horses. Lizzy considered herself very patient, and no doubt about it, she earned a gold star for her intentions. But it was not Baxter's job to help her achieve this patience. And it wasn't fair to him, or to her hopes for having a true equine partner, to be thinking, "He's got to change because I'm making this effort!" Her patience alone wouldn't guarantee that Baxter could resolve his stress about trailers. He was not one of those horses that seem to stay calm when their humans were unsettled. Each time Lizzy found her own place of calm, she could help Baxter get ready to feel okay about the trailer.

She was learning to give him some choice—not all the choices, but some, like the choice to say, "No, not now." And she was giving him the time he needed to settle and feel okay about what she was asking. Horses are capable of changing their minds when they know they are allowed to think and express their no before they let go of those thoughts and offer their yes.

Humming

Sandy was a round-bodied young adult who came to her weekly therapeutic riding lesson after a day in a structured program for people with disabilities. She was mute and avoided eye contact and touch. And although she always approached the mounting ramp in slow motion, she got on her horse Pal all by herself. She ignored the team's usual efforts to engage a rider: saying hello, asking how her day had been, giving her verbal guidance for mounting and asking Pal to "walk on." All these pleasantries we took for granted made her stiffen, look off, and lean away. She seemed to want more space between herself and us. Because she was well-balanced and had good gross motor skills, we granted her this space, letting her ride without the hands-on support from sidewalkers that many riders needed.

If she was excited to be riding again each week, it didn't show on her face. But she showed us her preferences through her actions—lying back over Pal's rump after she mounted. I welcomed her to ride this way: receptive and floating in the warmth and rhythm of Pal's walk. She looked peaceful when she heard only the sounds of wind, Pal's footsteps on the hard-packed arena footing, and the murmur of volunteers making small talk, while I directed the horse leader where to go and when to turn, stop, and walk on again.

I suspected that being in the day program was a significant

stressor for her, and I wanted her riding lessons to be a relief from that. I let her determine when and how and how much she would interact. Each week I did my best to assess her readiness for more overt social contact, then proceeded to gently nudge a bit here and there in an effort to expand her capacity to engage despite the stress. If she started to look around, I said, "Hi. Good to see you today." If she started stirring from the lying down position she favored, I said, "Sandy, are you ready to sit up?" Once she was sitting, I asked, "Would you hold the reins for a count of ten?"

I know from my own experience that a lot happens on the inside of a person who rides in this position on a calm, balanced horse. The calmness and the rhythm of the horse's walk seeps into the rider, bringing a sense of peace to the nervous system. This was Sandy's time to downshift from the state of distress after a day full of others' expectations—expectations to be in a room with other people, expectations to tolerate noise and activity, expectations to follow a schedule.

I waited for the inevitable: Sandy humming to herself. Quiet little humming sounds, like a young animal just starting to try out its voice. I started to hum, too. At first, I played follow-the-leader with her. She hummed a little riff, and I did my best version of repeating that—tone and tempo and volume. Her responses varied at different times in the lesson and from week to week. My unspoken questions were, "Is this a way we can be together?" and, "Are you okay to connect in this way or do you still want time and space without any requests for relating?"

She would go into a mini-freeze if she didn't want anyone to ask anything of her. She would stop humming. She would change her body position to be a bit further away from where I was walking near Pal's hind end, near where she rested her head and neck and torso. Now and then she would respond to my following her with another humming riff. These were super sweet moments.

Usually, she offered the same quality of sound, and at times she initiated a change, as if to check if I was really there and would follow her subtle shift. I could see and feel a softening in her body when those moments occurred. We were having a humming conversation. A call and response. She was calling, and I was responding in a way that allowed her to stay open to our contact. Delicate, open, tentative.

Once these moments of nonverbal connection occurred, she would sit up and practice basic riding skills, like holding the reins and looking in the direction of where we were going to next: the blue cone at the far end of the arena, or the red beanbag waiting on a fence post. She would transition at her own pace from the calming and regulating interactions, to engaging with skill-building activities.

Communication

Horses need to know how to get along well in our human world. Our responsibility is to teach them to stay back from electric fencing and find the water trough and stand quietly for the veterinarian. Central to teaching horses is communicating clearly and in ways they understand. While we are learning how to interpret their body language, they are learning ours as well. I'm still working on being better about my responsibilities and how I communicate.

Communication includes both expressing oneself and being heard and understood. It doesn't count if what I want to say to you isn't understood. Even words of the English language spoken by two native speakers are confusing with their multiple meanings and usages, which vary by region and culture. Type "confusing English language" into your favorite search engine for some chuckles and gasps. It's even more complex when we humans want to communicate with nonverbal species, like our horse friends.

When we think our horses are misbehaving, we communicate differently than when we pause to wonder what's driving the behavior we don't like. This pause allows us to interrupt our own habitual responses, and move away from reactivity toward curiosity. If the behavior is not caused by pain, then it's often due to a misunderstanding, a lack of understanding, or a miscommunication. By observing carefully when they're telling us no, we might understand that they can't do something because they don't have the skills or are in pain. We can help them rather than blame, criticize, or punish them. Helping them means I must attend diligently to my own self-regulation in order to insert a pause into my own reactivity. I want to send and receive messages that make sense to both of us. I may need to question myself rather than question my horse. "What can I do today to maintain connection with compassion even when I'm scared, angry, or otherwise upset?"

With people, I can neutralize the impact of their words by intentionally reframing or restating what they have said, often making explicit their emotional undertones. With children, I tend to be direct, hoping to educate them about emotions. A young rider was upset at his horse and said, "I hate you, Champ!"

I responded, "You sound really mad about what Champ just did." (With an adult, I might say, "I wonder if you have a word for the emotion you're feeling right now.")

Another young rider frowned at me, narrowing her eyes and saying, "You are old and ugly. You must be three hundred years old."

I responded, "You sound kinda mad at me." Inviting more expression, I asked, "Would you like to tell me more?"

An instructor colleague questioned my choices with Sandy, asking, "Couldn't she be practicing her riding skills? She knows enough to steer independently."

I responded, "First things first. I'm willing to wait for her to be ready, and that includes being settled enough to make the choice to hold the reins, not just be compliant with my directions."

Some of the therapy horses I've met had a pause, the ability to wait quietly for more direction—very useful for those times when an instructor or horse leader needed to think for a moment about what to say or do next. Some horses have virtually no pause, so any millisecond of straying human attention results in the horse taking initiative. Not good for a lesson setting.

A horse like Baxter is not trying to get away with things, nor take advantage of us. Those are human concepts that don't match what motivates the horse. The horse sees when we are not alert, attentive, and responsible in our decision-making role, and then does what is natural—makes choices based on self-preservation.

As part of my social work education, I interned in Child Protective Services. There I learned about physical abuse and neglect. We were expected to intervene when there were broken bones, but broken spirits were overlooked. The needs of the neglected went unattended by service agencies and funding policies. We child protective workers felt helpless and depressed about those children who "slipped through the cracks." Passing over the neglected children in order to prevent more broken bones was the hardest part of that job. And so here I am ensconced in my personal and professional roles (psychotherapist and therapeutic riding instructor) and trying to heal the impact of neglect, part of the broad umbrella of developmental trauma.

With horses, abuse is obvious—such as when someone hurts or scares a horse with whip, spurs, ropes, sticks, chains, or gunshot. Or confines a horse with no access to food or water, shade or shelter. But leaving a horse mentally confused? Is that abuse? That opens up a new realm of wondering, leading me to ask, "What am I doing that confuses a horse? What am I doing that leaves a horse experiencing this type of abuse?"

I had a few conversations with horsemanship clinician Harry Whitney about gray areas and maybes. I was struggling to understand this notion that horses thrive on black and white, on communications that leave no questions. That this type of clarity supports a horse's well-being. I can't have a conversation full of maybes and "it depends"—not with horses at least. Humans waffle. I had the habit of changing my mind mid-sentence, even changing direction mid-stride. This erratic behavior doesn't work around horses. I suspect if I were a horse acting that way in a herd, they would run me off, because my behavior would be a threat to the herd's survival.

Safety was my number-one priority when I taught therapeutic riding lessons. If all of a sudden I perceived danger, keeping the riders and volunteers safe was more important to me than communicating well. I raised my voice to interrupt what was happening. I wasn't fond of getting upset during a lesson, but I would follow up with an apology, hoping to reduce whatever upset I had passed along. "I'm sorry I raised my voice. I saw Wally tossing his head close to your head, and I got scared. I had to say something right away and I probably scared you when I raised my voice. I'm sorry I scared you, but I wanted to make sure you would be safe right then and there. I wanted to keep you from getting whacked in the head."

Misinterpreting communications is common even when two people speak the same language. It's even easier to misinterpret when we're speaking as different species with our different ways of communicating. I remember at home with my herd, I came to the field carrying a halter in order to bring my horse Kacee into the barn to do something together. Watching her walk away left me thinking she didn't want anything to do with me. I finally paused myself long enough to notice that she was walking away to poop, before coming to join me.

When I realized Kacee was simply getting ready to meet with me, I applied this lesson to my own life. I wanted to understand why people could communicate so well at times and so poorly at times. I learned that when stress increases to the point where our flight/fight response takes over, we lose connection with our higher-thinking brains. Same with the horses. If they are in a reactive mode, a state of high sympathetic activation, they can't access what they've been learning. What they need is understanding and patience and guidance to settle and return to feeling safe. Once safe, their best thinking and their ability to learn are available. Think about Baxter learning to be close to the trailer. He needed to feel safe before he could consider approaching the trailer. Just like us.

Horses and humans have the same needs to feel safe in relationships. In order to communicate well with others, I keep returning to strengthening this direct connection with myself in the fullest, most embodied ways possible. Mindful movement, conscious breathing, and intentional quieting of my busy mind when I'm with people or animals—these are my personal access routes for connecting with myself. From here I can adapt to the shifting contrasts of certainty and not knowing. The spiritual directive to "Be Here Now" with no preconceptions—"beginner's mind" in martial arts—contradicts our need for predictability. Where is the line between routine and novelty? Horses need both. We need both. All mammalian nervous systems need both stimulation and rest. We're looking for a dynamic balance of these two, but there are no maps telling us exactly which routes will take us there.

CHAPTER 11

Learning

Being with horses is simple if our goal is to promote a calm state of mind when we are together, and through all the tasks we ask of them. If we can habitually help a horse reach a calm and quiet state of mind, that state carries over to other tasks.
— CRISSI MCDONALD

AT THE SCRATCHING CONE

FINALLY. Weather and mood and stars lined up for me to leave the house and head out to the horses with the possibility of playfulness leading the way.

Rusty sauntered in my direction as I arrived carrying an orange cone, a floppy blue foam pool noodle, and a purple nylon flag attached to the end of a stiff wire rod.

He touched everything with his nose and then turned to chewing on the pool noodle, rendering it into two pieces, disqualifying it as a free-access play toy. Assessment complete, he resumed munching whatever itsy bits of early spring grass he could find.

Needing a plan, I decided to see if I could communicate to Rusty that I'd scratch his belly if he touched the cone. Scratches were divine since the arrival of black flies, mosquitos, and who-knows-what other biting annoyances left him eager for relief. I knew he would be motivated once he figured this out.

Based on some things I'd learned in a presentation about teaching therapeutic riding to autistic people with varying support needs, I interacted with Rusty as if he were a human student with moderately severe auditory processing difficulties. That meant I worked hard to express my ideas in ways he could hear and understand. I was pleased that I didn't once get frustrated or angry, and if you are wondering why I would even mention this, I had had plenty of moments marred by gritted teeth and irritation directed at my very own beloved horses—but not so with my students or the horses at the therapeutic riding program where I taught. Somehow, I managed my emotions better in public than at home.

My changed approach was effective with Rusty. When he didn't understand what I was asking, I asked differently, in a simpler way. My goals were to help him find the answer and remain patient while he was trying. When he seemed to "get it" and then not get it, I brought my attention to feeling my own feet on the ground and softened my belly. This helped me calm myself, and then I sought an even simpler way to ask. He responded slo-o-o-o-o-owly to these smaller requests from me. Which meant he was thinking as fast as he could, which was slo-o-o-o-o-ow, because he's a horse and I would always win a processing-speed contest based on my prefrontal cortex versus his. Other speed contests—like speed of reflexes and movement—I would lose.

I restrained the habitual compulsion to repeat, repeat, repeat my requests, as if hammering him with the same question would bring a different answer. When he found his way to touching the cone and looking to me for the scratching three times in a row, I gave him his final scratching with thanks in my heart for his interest in engaging with me. I gathered the orange and blue and purple objects and started back to the barn.

One of Rusty's herd-mates, Sofia, had been watching us and came to greet me. Hmmm. I wondered if she would like to play the same game. She was touching the cone with her curiosity in a jiffy—my cue to start scratching. She liked this. Her extended quivering upper lip was a clear giveaway of her pleasure.

I stopped scratching and moved the cone off to the left. She reached for it, nudged it, and I started scratching again. This fun exchange went on until Rusty wandered over and asked Sofia to move in typical Rusty fashion (*"MOVE! NOW!"*) before he lowered his head and touched the cone with his muzzle. Me? Scratch, scratch, scratch. I moved the cone a few feet ahead, aware that this would test his understanding of our game. He took a wee glance in my direction and then stepped forward to the cone and touched it. And I resumed my scratching.

All in all, it was a very successful experiment and a very remedial chunk of horse time for me. Horse time is healing time when I am calm and enjoying our activities. This horse time included a glimpse of how easily Rusty learns and how willing he is to help me learn more about the intelligence of a horse.

I'm Learning

It had been a few weeks since I'd ridden. Maybe closer to many weeks. The chilly spring rains in Vermont might have kept me from riding anyway, but in fact I had been grounded because of injuries. I had sustained my injuries falling off a horse, and I grew determined to first get together mentally with any horse I wanted to ride by doing groundwork. So far, I'd kept to my word.

That day I rode the smallest equine I had at home, and the biggest.

The smallest was Gwen, a dappled grey Shetland pony. I never rode her long or far because of her size, only a little here and there to assess and expand her understanding of the riding experience. I wanted to prepare her to go live with a neighboring family whose young daughter had caught the horse bug.

Gwen would have lots of the little-girl-grooming-and-loving attention she so adored. I hoped the match would be good so Gwen would live there happily ever after. If not, I'd promised Gwen she would come back to my herd. This matched the agreement made with my neighbors: Gwen would come back to me if things didn't work out for any reason. Free pony with a guaranteed take-back plan in place. Who could refuse?

Sofia was my biggest equine—a black, half-Percheron mare, impressive at sixteen hands—the equivalent of five and a half feet tall as measured at the withers—and glorified by her long wavy mane and tail. And irksome with her partial attention as I lunged her before bringing her to the mounting block. She did not come close enough to the block for me to mount her, which was her way of saying, "I might have some other ideas about what we'll be doing." Instead of repositioning her so she'd be closer, or moving the block to where she stood, I decided to do something else. Off with the halter and back to lunging, this time at liberty, without halter and lunge line.

Once we were circling together with smooth transitions from walking to trotting then back to walking, I asked her to come with me to the block again. This time she came fully into place for me to mount. After a short bareback ride, I dismounted and gave her lots of scratches—and hanging out time.

I had thought I might ride Rusty as well. But, true to my commitment, I first focused on improving our groundwork, those unmounted activities that help build connection. My goal that day was walking and trotting at liberty, with him in tune and comfortable with my requests.

Rusty and I played the Scratching Cone game again. When I asked him to go for a walk with me, he stayed focused on getting scratched. It was hard for him to switch gears, so I put the cone outside the pen and then asked him again to go for a walk with me. Even without the cone, Rusty was thinking about how to position himself so I could keep scratching his belly. So many bug bites! He would walk off a few steps at my request and then turn to come close again for scratches. When I put some distance between us, he moved to the platform and stepped up—a sure way to get more scratches, yes? But no, I had not asked for that, so I waited for him to do something different. When he stepped down, he looked around for some grass to nibble; apparently I didn't know how to play this game properly, so he chose to occupy himself while I figured things out.

I got his attention again, asking him to move out while I was walking at his hip. We had some nice walks and changes of direction, but the added life and understanding to move into a trot just wasn't there. It was a classic picture: human putting out a lot of effort, horse putting out minimal effort. I decided I didn't want to keep doing this and headed for the pen gate.

As I left the pen, Rusty followed. I picked up the cone and tossed it a few feet away, hoping to draw Rusty's attention for more scratching and end on a good note.

A light went off in my little brain! After he earned and received his scratching, I tossed the cone as far as I could, headed toward it with Rusty at my side, and asked him to trot with me. Trot we did, right up to the cone where he nose-dived it and waited for his scratches, which I gladly gave.

I can be slow to learn. But I did learn to use what works to set up a situation for success. Rusty would go to the cone for scratches. I wanted him to trot with me at liberty. Throw the cone and ask him to trot to it with me. We repeated this five times on the way to the back door of the barn. Thank you, Rusty. It seemed so simple once I realized it.

Distrust and Belief

I was teaching Rusty how to load into my gray, CM bumper-pull ramp-load trailer. It was the first time I was trying to do so without his buddy Kacee already in the trailer, because I was short on time and didn't want to spend the usual hour convincing her to get into the trailer. I was taking a chance asking Rusty to step in without his buddy there waiting.

It took quite a few tries. He had several successful avoidant moves: to the right, to the left, and standing stock still, refusing to step forward toward the ramp.

I had fewer moves, as this was during an early stage of my horsemanship skill-building. I knew how to pull, push, and get really, really frustrated to the point of raising my voice, pleading, and crying.

Eventually, I stopped and stood there. Even though I'd seen all those pressure and release techniques demonstrated, I was unable to replicate what others had done. Okay, how about I try to picture what I want in my mind's eye, and then ask Rusty nicely? I included assuring him that once he went in easily, we'd be done.

Rusty walked up the ramp and into the trailer.

I was stunned and excited and didn't really believe what had happened.

So after backing him out of the trailer, I asked him to go in again. I wanted proof that it wasn't just an accident that he went in. Poor choice. Another half hour of my frustration, Rusty's frustration and refusals, and unpleasant feelings between us growing with each attempt.

Then came my "aha" moment. I'd promised him we'd be done, and I'd broken my promise. Yeah, if this was all a bunch of malarkey, this talking to your horse, then it didn't really matter whether I promised him something or not. But if that was what actually made a difference, then indeed I'd offended him, shown my distrust of him and what he understands and is capable of doing in response to my requests.

I apologized and asked him to do it once more just because I'm a stupid human and then, really and truly, we'd be done. "I'm sorry but this is what I need in order to believe you, Rusty."

And he walked into the trailer. And I cried. Ashamed and grateful all bundled up together.

The Tank Challenge

Petra was my first equine challenge as a therapeutic riding instructor-in-training. She was a Norwegian Fjord horse who moved like a tank without brakes. Her unstoppable forward motion was welcome when we wanted to go someplace but was a problem when she was asked to stop. Here was another therapy horse with a reputation for being difficult.

There were volunteers on hand to help with lessons, but none offered to lead Petra. I needed to figure out how to lead her myself while teaching. Fortunately, my young student Sam had enough strength and balance to ride while I focused on convincing Petra to walk and turn and stop. I'll brag that I was successful enough, which means although we seldom stopped within a few steps after my request to stop, we always stopped within a few yards of my request.

Volunteers were scarce for sidewalking, as I said, when it was time for a lesson with Petra. After checking with the program director about safety policy and protocol, I enlisted Sam's eager mother to join the therapeutic riding team and help provide the safe-enough lesson. It went well.

I had multiple roles in this lesson with Sam and Petra: instructor, horse leader, volunteer trainer, horse trainer, volunteer manager, and parent-child coach. In the serene setting at that facility, and with my quiet determination and large store of creative adaptations, Sam benefitted despite the unusual arrangements. He rode, he played games while riding, and he practiced using the reins and his voice for stopping.

I had been told that a chain over Petra's nose was the only way to stop her. I'd watched others lead her this way, which meant relying on pain to get her attention and cooperation. And if someone was hurting a horse to communicate successfully, it hurt me to witness—and I couldn't truly consider it successful communication.

I had a few different strategies in mind for communicating without the chain pain, so I came to work early each week and spent time with Petra before the lesson. I wanted to find out how to engage her brain instead of trying to control her strong body. I wanted to transform her lack of interest in what was being asked of her. I wanted to interrupt her certainty that humans didn't understand or honor her needs—a mindset likely behind much of her "pushiness," as it was called. Of course, she could stop without great pressure from her handler. I knew this because I'd seen her act like any horse would. Out in a pasture, she regularly stopped and walked and stopped again.

It was a matter of a communication gap. And my job was to figure out how to communicate, "Let's stop, Petra. I won't use force. I'll help you understand what I want." Using my breathing, slowing my own pace and energy level, I modeled what I wanted her to do, inviting her to join me in these changes. Which she did.

Learning

In my quest to learn about equine-facilitated services, I have spent time with horsewomen dually trained as educators and therapists. I've attended conferences and educational retreats, both as a student and a presenter. I continue to seek to know more about our horses and more about becoming a better human for my horses. I have spent time in dance studios and bodywork sessions, and on the mats of yoga and Aikido classes. I have spent time learning about trauma in humans and trauma in horses, and countless hours over countless years in my own therapy, unraveling the stuck places that have kept me from being my best version of me.

My curiosity always centered on the relationships between humans and horses. Good horsemanship is based on good relationships. The quality of horsemanship that is possible depends on the quality of relationship one aspires to.

Some horsemanship clinicians have excellent reputations based on the help they offer horses, but not all have excellent reputations for how they interact with people. When I'm presented with a lesson that is unclear or that comes with a frown, a sense of urgency, or a raised voice, I can imagine what my horse might experience being trained by someone like that. We gain empathy for our horses' experiences when we slow down, feel, and acknowledge what we are experiencing when we ourselves are being led into unknown territory as part of a learning curve.

At this point in my life, if I don't feel safe with someone, it doesn't matter what they have to offer. I don't want to spend time and money learning from that person. It's an effort to separate *what* I'm learning from *how* I'm learning. I don't want to feel defensive while I'm learning. Any communication that leaves me feeling intimidated, put down, belittled, or talked down to creates a situation where I am suffering the other person's dysregulation—even if I'm sure that person is also suffering.

On the other hand, I'm ready and willing to experience the uncomfortable feelings that accompany struggling to understand something. This type of discomfort is a regular part of my learning experience, as when I was figuring out how to get Rusty to trot with me.

I'm grateful that I have access to teachers who use generous doses of humor and kindness as they present new ideas or give me feedback. I need these—not messages of inadequacy—especially when I start feeling shame, realizing I've been insensitive and have confused my horses.

Teachers are not better than I am just because they know something I don't know yet. I'm not better than my horses because I am a human with different capacities for intellectual knowledge. May I be kept humble when it's me facilitating people as they're learning. I may know something about horses that they don't, but I'll never know more than they do about the aspects of life in their areas of expertise. As a teacher, I want to adjust to suit the students' wants and needs, not have them adjust to mine. I like the image of instructor as servant. Same with horses. I am their servant when I'm helping them learn.

Most of my life I've been comfortable following others in the compliant roles of child or student. It's equally important to me to be effective in the teacher role when I'm with my horses. Can I be a teacher who supports the dignity and integrity of the horses?

A good teacher offers clarity, choice, and mutuality. A teacher of horses must offer these qualities within the limitations of what we can provide while keeping our horses in captivity. In most cultures, we can have horses with us because they are captive. This status has its benefits and challenges. Petra had a job to fulfill in the captivity setting of a therapeutic riding program, and I did my best to help her do it with more understanding and ease.

Training horses entails making decisions and preparing the horses for learning; helping them understand our requests and what our cues mean; and letting them know we value their calm physiological states more than their performances.

I want to eliminate the horses' need to question whether I am friend or foe. For horses to count on me as the calm person they can turn to when worry arises, I need to be consistent in mood and action. Horses want to survive and feel safe, and we want to feel safe and enjoy our time with them. I struggled with this as I was introducing Rusty to my trailer-loading expectations. My angst added to his confusion, until I realized how clear I needed to be with him. Not forceful, but clear.

Being proactive and mindful of what the horse knows how to do will help keep us safe. We may not like what the horse chooses to do when we leave that to him, such as lie down and roll on the sandy beach where we're riding. So, we are faced with a conundrum: How can I give my horse choice while providing myself with the best chance for being safe?

We can easily and inadvertently demean horses in our efforts to train them. Teaching them to do things for our pleasure is a version of trick training. I'm not sure what the right word would be for this—for when we involve horses in activities that suit our human ideas of what they should do. Maybe we are doing it for entertainment, for a sense of popularity, uniqueness, or superiority, or for a challenge. Such training seldom helps the horse be comfortable as a horse living in our human environment. It's not the horse's job to entertain us. It's similar to trick-training children. I was trained as a child to smile and curtsy to each adult, one by one, around the living room during my parents' cocktail parties. A circle of big people, and scared little me with no choice to say no.

What about the horses? Why is it important that we develop the qualities of good teachers? When we are their herd, it's up to us to furnish the calmness if we expect them to relax with us. Our physical and emotional energy will impact the horse. Vibes speak louder than words. Think of a herd—one horse notices something, and the rest of the herd reacts immediately. This is how our horses live. They read our vibes, respond to our vibes, and feel safe with us or confused by us. They try desperately to get along with us despite our vibes. My intention is to treat my horses with honor regarding this aspect of their beings. I also intend to learn to treat myself with the same honor, although this has been harder. I keep learning more about integrity and kindness from time spent with horses.

Being in a learning frame of mind depends on having choices. What choices do our horses have when they live in captivity? What choices do we want them to have? Can we accommodate their having more choices even if it means changing our horse-care habits and lifestyle choices?

When we give horses choices instead of telling them what to do, they will choose what makes them feel safe and comfortable. And they need to have an understanding of what's expected. Central to everything we do, we best serve our horses when we ask again and again, "What can I do to help you, Horse?"

CHAPTER 12

Paying Attention

To pay attention, this is our endless and proper work.
— Mary Oliver

Winter Practice

It was winter in New Hampshire. Snow. Cold. Sun. Clouds. Cold. Mild. Cold. Really, really cold. I had just moved to my new home and the horses were there, too, settling in. I loved seeing them through the window in the morning. They knew where to stand so they could see movement inside the house, anticipating my coming out to feed them hay.

I was getting more cardiovascular exercise since the move. The hay was stored up top of a fairly steep, snow-covered incline, and the gate to the horses' paddock was a bit of a walk further. As my body got stronger, I began to practice some Aikido between carrying bales to the horses. All decked out in my blue quilted construction suit and sheepskin hat and double-layered mittens, there at the end of the indoor riding arena where the hay was stacked.

It felt like I was endowing the building with some special energy each time I did this. I envisioned this as an altar in motion, a proper acknowledgement of the spiritual side of my horsemanship.

This winter activity was developing my awareness with centering and grounding movement patterns I'd been learning in Mark Rashid's Aikido for Horsemen clinics (now called Aibado), and from Aikido practice at a local dojo. Although I wasn't riding regularly, I could practice daily. Practice paying attention, carrying myself efficiently, gaining emotional resilience and physical strength, and integrating into my everyday life activities the wonderful morsels I gained each time I meditated and each time I invested in a clinic where my horsemanship and personal growth shared the focus.

Life was good. There were painful moments, yes, and energetic moments, tired moments, busy moments, quiet moments. Through it all ran a thread of increasing calm and acceptance. And I loved the possibility of bringing these qualities to my horses.

What Is It?

Rusty was certain there was a bear in the woods. His gaze fixated beyond the arena fence that contained us both. His attention was hijacked as we stood side by side. I no longer existed. I'd seldom seen him this wound up—tail high as he stood frozen, sounding the honk-snort that horses do. Their alarm system. My plan to ride him for a third time that day came to a halt.

Why would I ride him three times? The first would be my normal feel-him-out and warm-him-up ride. If all went well in my comfy, secure-feeling About the Horse western saddle, I'd try out my new Bates Isabell dressage saddle.

Rusty had some of his predictable, athletic vertical liveliness of the bouncy bucky sort, but not so much that I stiffened in fear. I suspected the crusty, snow-covered chunky frozen sand in the arena added to his discomfort. After twenty minutes of brisk walk, bunched-up trot, and teeter-totter canter, we headed back to the barn to change saddles.

I adorned the dressage saddle with a grab strap, just-in-case-thank-you-very-much, and led him back to the arena, where I mounted. Walking was fine. Trotting was extremely bunched up and short-strided. Then he moved into some major bucks—time and time again. My ride-a-buck balance was elusive in that saddle, and a couple of times I wondered if I was getting dislodged beyond my ability to come back to the saddle. Yuck. Bone-rattling, breathtaking, heart-pounding yuck. Scarier than I like.

I dismounted in one of those brief pauses between bucking and felt instant comfort as my feet connected with the ground. I removed Rusty's bridle and let him loose, wondering, "Why all the bucking today?" This was more than his usual bounding and bouncing—this was bucking and kicking out with effort. Poor saddle fit was the prime suspect, but I was still running through other possible culprits. I thought about riding him again in the western saddle to confirm or rule out the Bates saddle as buck-maker. But remember the bear? Yeah, that prompted my decision to stay with my feet on the ground—one of my wisest survival strategies around horses.

I continued my mental review of what could have caused the bucking. I'm pretty sure the Bates saddle interfered with his shoulders, but darn, I loved the feel of it. The uneven footing unbalanced him, threatening his stability and mobility. The bear was lurking in the woods all afternoon. The moon was practically full. Any other educated suggestions or wild guesses?

As much as I criticize those who *oooh* and *aaah* at the appearance of a very scared horse—head high, eyes wide, nostrils flaring, tail flagged—I confess some part of me enjoyed seeing Rusty in his heightened state of sympathetic activation. I was very glad I was not still riding him. I much preferred observing his awesome athletic maneuvers with my feet on the ground.

Hurry to Here

There was so much beauty surrounding me where I lived on the fringe of New Hampshire's White Mountains. Wild turkeys roaming the fields. Songbirds calling amongst themselves. Tree limbs reaching into the sky. To the west, the sunset outlined the mountains. I paused to take this in, settling into the simple rightness of nature. No need to close my eyes and visualize—the beauty was right there for me to experience.

Well, most of the time.

That morning I was reminded of other aspects of this locale. Cold. Rain. Ice lurking under puddles of manure soup. Me cringing from any contact with the dripping wet farm animals I love to touch.

A part of me took this in, as I did the beauty.

A part of me was grateful that I had anticipated the slippery footing and had struggled to secure ice cleats over my barn boots.

A part of me carried on with the chores while a part of me rushed through them as quickly as possible, eager to be elsewhere, hurrying to be warm and dry inside the house.

This hurry is what causes trouble.

Hurry meant I might stumble on a piece of frozen manure, or get tilted off balance by sheep crowding me as I carried hay. Hurry might mean the manure I was shoveling fell to the ground, not into the wheelbarrow. Sometimes it meant I stood there in frustration, swearing at a bale of hay that refused to be dislodged from the stack.

The common thread in these scenarios? Me. Me, when I am inattentive. Me, when I am unsettled. Me, when I am misattuned to the actual conditions of my environment.

Inside again, warm and dry and safe from the dangers of the barn on a cold, rainy day, I further pondered the nature of hurry and how it is a problem.

Hurry lures me out of this present moment, drawing me into a state of disconnection. It is well-endowed with restlessness and discontent. It steals my attention from what is and locks it into what isn't. These what-isn't places are familiar and reliable, residing in the past and in the future.

I confess a certain infatuation with the past and the future. These two are infinitely entertaining and permit me the satisfaction of choice. I can let my mind wander anywhere, into leisurely reminiscing or hope-infused fantasizing. Even when haunted by painful memories and perilous predictions, I am enchanted.

My cozy relationship with the past and future stems from devoted practice as a self-improvement enthusiast, one who works diligently toward a future self, imagined as more whole, more capable, more confident, more loving, more productive, more worthy. This rambling around the past and the future seems a good-enough use of my currently available life energy. Well, maybe a pretty lousy use of it, except perhaps when I'm weaving tales with my beloved wordsmith cap snug on my head.

The past and the future are rich for those of us in a love relationship with our memories and imaginations. That richness is infused with images, narratives, emotions, and all the externally- and internally-oriented senses. We have this amazing capacity to create movies with our minds—and respond to them—without ever moving a muscle. These movies are what mesmerize me, bringing me through an unending series of experiential states, followed by an unending commentary in the quest for making meaning.

And what happens to this wealth of past and future when I don't hurry? What happens then?

These mind movies morph and evoke a different response. In some moments—very precious moments—the mind movies pause, and I am void of conflicts and aspirations, simply being me: the breathing, sensing version of me.

Tears moistened my eyes then as I absorbed the pinks and purples and oranges and grays that graced the evening sky. Tears of release, not loss, flowed as I shifted from hurry to here. I rested from all that wandering through the past and the future and settled into stillness.

These still moments are alive with something so potent and elusive. I find myself serenely experiencing through my senses. My heart beats, and my lungs breathe, and my eyes see, and my ears hear, and my nose smells, and my skin feels.

In the absence of hurry is this fullness of what is.

Practicing Softness

I started out the day cranky. I had made a commitment to paint some of the pine boards that would become the new kitchen ceiling and turned down an invitation to ride with a friend who lived about two miles away. Preparing to paint, I gathered a paintbrush, set four boards on each set of sawhorses, pried open a gallon of the off-white paint with a screwdriver, and stirred before dipping my paintbrush in. My mind was heavy with reluctance to be doing what I was doing. Then I remembered hearing Mark Rashid say, "You get good at what you practice."

Along with that phrase came other memories about developing softness, whatever you are doing. There I was, painting and remembering softness. What an opportunity. Even though I wasn't with my horses on a sunny afternoon, I could work on the most important things I could ever hope to bring to my horses: softness, presence, and awareness.

The time passed quickly. I tested my balance and strength by painting while standing on one foot, switching feet every minute or so. I finished all the boards I had ready, and then shifted gears while the paint dried. I headed out to the horses, intending a long trail ride, and after a brief deliberation about which horse to ride and where, I chose my Morgan mare, Kacee.

I had been fantasizing about taking Kacee to an upcoming clinic with Mark Rashid. I imagined asking him for help to get me from where I was with her, to where I wanted to be—which was to go out for a trail ride whenever I wanted to. My goal seemed elusive because Kacee grew anxious when separated from the other horses. Several things came together for me that day. First the practice of softness, then whatever it was that got me ready to *just go do it*—just go ride the trail with Kacee.

I had been practicing breathing consciously while I groomed and tacked her, and then again in the ring for our time warming up and getting more connected. I breathed long and slow, deliberately exhaling for longer than I inhaled. I did all this while walking and trotting and walking, walking, walking. I continued this practice into my trail ride. Perhaps that was the foundation of my success, side by side with softness. I breathed. I focused. I directed Kacee and I kept experimenting with how to direct her so that she was comfortable accepting my direction. Waiting for her to change her mind when she hesitated. Me focusing on breathing instead of me holding my breath and getting frustrated.

I came home feeling proud of myself.

On some level it seemed like such a small thing—to go for a trail ride with Kacee. But there was nothing small about that with our history of her reluctance to leave the herd and then her out-of-control galloping back to the barn, coupled with my inability to slow myself in order to help her settle.

So, I had succeeded with my trail riding goal with Kacee. I was left wondering, what help would I ask for at the clinic?

Learning to Soften

Manley was my all-time favorite therapy horse. This heart connection grew from my involvement with bringing him to our therapy program. The online description of a sound, middle-aged, experienced lesson and trail horse caught my attention. Seeing his photo clinched it for me—one of those vivid *Yes!* moments. I passed along his information and my encouragement to Allison, our horse herd coordinator, and hoped she would deem him a good fit. Manley arrived by trailer a few weeks later, joining the herd for a one-month trial period to see if he would settle and feel okay with us and our particular set of equine job expectations.

The cold New England winter months meant no lessons for our usual riders. I had plenty of time to get to know Manley and help assess him as a riding horse, a leadline horse, and a stand-around-and-be-loved-on horse, and see where he might need more support in order to fit in as a therapy horse.

I had volunteered to bring my horse-training skills to the herd. My passion was to help horses like Manley understand just how easy it can be to walk on, whoa, turn left and right, wait at the mounting block, and be calm when toys (like beanbags used for games on horseback) are tossed over his back. I enjoyed riding his smooth walk, trot, and canter, and I enjoyed his temperament. Manley was consistently calm and in an attentive, learning frame of mind.

And he was braced. That was the first thing I addressed. I'm referring to his habit of stiffness through his body, a stiffness that got stronger when pressure was applied through the reins. Bracing in the neck is a common pattern for a horse, as it helps them protect against pressure on the mouth. But it means the horse is stiff and less than welcoming of contact with the rider. Riding a braced horse feels like riding a cross between an 8x8 beam and an actual horse.

I knew Manley could soften because I knew any horse could soften. I knew he could respond to gentle requests because I knew that any horse could. My job was to ask softly, ask consistently, and notice how he responded, waiting for him to soften into the softness I offered. My job was also to let him know when he was softening by softening even more myself. This softening was how I communicated yes to his responses to my questions: "Could you soften this brace a bit, Manley?" Or, "Can you meet me here in this soft contact?"

Manley increasingly met my requests with softness. He was curious and willing, offering this quality once he understood his softness was welcomed as a gift, not demanded of him. He discovered it felt better to be soft than to be braced, and I did my best not to give him any reasons to protect himself when we were together. As lessons resumed in early spring, I returned to my instructor role and a mix of staff and volunteers started handling and riding him as part of his life as a lesson horse. This quality of softness we had enjoyed was not recognized or sought by the others. Not out of meanness—just less awareness of what Manley needed from us. He returned to bracing. His need for protective responses made sense to me. But it hurt to watch his vulnerability retreat.

Any softness or bracing happens within the relationship. Recognizing that prompted me to offer trainings based on experiential education. I hoped staff and volunteers would find their own softness and understand how it benefits the horses when that is what we offer. It takes a team effort to change the mindset and the embodied habits in order to help it become the default way of being for horses like Manley.

It was hard not only watching his softness disappear, but also watching riders and volunteers become frustrated and even feel threatened by Manley. I regretted that I wasn't able to follow through on his behalf and that he had to resort to self-protection with those stiffer, more braced responses to people's requests.

An easy way to ensure that any therapeutic riding horse retains responsiveness and interest in interacting when questions are asked of him, by people who could receive his answers, would be to limit who handled him and offer regular training and support to these handlers. I worked once at a therapeutic riding center where the horse handlers were paid staff assigned to the same horses in the same lessons week after week. Those horses fared well emotionally and physically, and performed reliably because they knew their handlers and how requests were communicated. They did not need to adjust to new handlers in every lesson. This made for happier horses. That therapy program was organized—well organized—around inclusion of volunteers as sidewalkers. I valued this tremendously and knew how much it meant to the volunteers from my own experience of volunteering in a therapeutic riding program, years before I became an instructor. We never found a way to meld the two there where Manley lived and worked—balancing the involvement of many volunteers in a busy day of lessons with the needs of the horses to know their handlers and have a familiar routine with familiar expectations.

Meanwhile, Manley remained my favorite. Our connection carried into my lesson time instructing a student on Manley. Even though a leader led him or a rider directed him from his back, Manley would tune in to me across the ring for assurance and direction. This kind of connection is invisible to many people, but in full view of—and essential to—the horses.

I didn't always have this ability to recognize connection with a horse. I'm pretty sure I had it as a child when I spent long hours with the school horses at the Moffats' lesson barn. I helped catch the horses and bring them in from pasture. I fed them and mucked stalls. I groomed them. And I rode them. And as a child, the simple and untainted ability to be present and responsive was my innate *modus operandi*, especially with animals. Over the years, like Manley, I myself developed braces against this degree of openness.

Eventually I had to relearn how to soften. This relearning included years of therapy, bodywork, yoga, meditation, tears, trying and failing and trying again to be in relationships, and hours and hours with horses alone and in clinic settings with the best horsemanship teachers I could find. My interest in performing in the ring never matched my wanting to connect. I wanted to show up and sense in those nonverbal realms what was working and not working. I wanted to let go of my protective need to be stronger or wiser than the horses. I wanted to know my fear and relearn how to be flexible and strong and balanced through my core so I could go with the horse, not just ride on it and tell it what to do. I wanted to offer the insides of me to the insides of the horse.

If only this type of connection were easy to teach! It certainly has not been easy to learn. But it's the key to making things better for our horses, to be operating as an integrated inside/outside person when we're around horses. Well, when we're doing anything . . . not just when we're around horses. Thanks to hearing Mark Rashid talk about "softness as a way of life," I devoted myself to this as a way of life, not just a way of horsemanship.

Manley's Treatment Plan

Problems:
1. Potential for long-term joint damage and pain with ewe-necked, sway-backed posture.

2. Pushes into pressure, failure to yield or give way.
3. Shortened reach with left hind when bending to the left.

Strengths:
1. Calm demeanor.
2. Steady gaits with variation within walk and trot.
3. Curious mind.

Objectives:
1. Re-educate how to carry himself softly to strengthen abdominal and hindquarter muscles and to relax topline muscles.
2. Develop the habit of yielding his ideas to those of his handler or rider.
3. Readily yield to pressure in all directions: forward, back, left, right, up, and down.

Actions:
1. Backing up to learn softness and engage hindquarters.
2. Backing up in an arc to strengthen and balance hindquarters.
3. Walk and trot with softness, in arcs and circles to balance strength on both sides.
4. Frequent transitions (halt-walk-halt, halt-trot-halt, walk-trot-walk) and changes of direction while being led or ridden to assess his current status regarding yielding of mind and body.
5. Belly scratches before, during, and/or after lessons to help him lift his back.
6. Offer him a release of pressure during or after a downward transition only when he relaxes and lowers head, if he doesn't do this automatically.

Implementation:
1. Who: herd coordinator, instructors, specifically identified volunteers.
2. How often: 3-5 times a week.
3. Length of each session: ½ to 1 hour.
4. For how long until reassessment: 4 weeks.

Assessments:
1. Head low during mounting, dismounting, coming to a halt.
2. Travels equally well to the left and to the right.
3. When being led, transitions into trotting without pushing on leader.
4. Readily responds to leader or rider requests for all activities.

Paying Attention

My love for horses has motivated me to be more aware of how they perceive the world—how they think and communicate, what emotions they are capable of, what they need, and how they get their needs met. My inquiries led me to wonder about perceived safety and lack of safety, companionship, play, responses to pressure, herd relationships, and interspecies nonverbal communications.

Perhaps that early life-threatening experience of being suffocated by my brother set the stage for me to be especially attentive to what's happening around me. I have worked to balance my hypervigilant external focus by connecting with my inner voice—those gut hunches, those words of wisdom coming from my heart that I dare to hear now. I consider it one of those possible gifts of trauma, finding a path that transforms terrifying events into useful skills and perceptions.

At this point I'm on automatic drive, running self-assessments all the time. Where's my attention? What am I feeling? What would help me feel better? How's my body? Where am I soft, tight? My toes? My jaw? Am I on a mission and mentally ahead of myself? Am I still and listening? How's my breathing? What happens when I pause? Does my breathing quicken or does it deepen? Am I moving efficiently from my core, with fluid joints, shoulders resting over my ribs? What are my eyes seeing? What part of me is steering this decision?

We humans and horses are wired to be on the lookout for change. Our survival depends on noticing what's around us, to determine if something is friend or foe. Rusty was obvious in his focus on the woods that may have housed a threatening bear.

Our survival also depends on being aware of what's happening inside us—our sensations, emotions, thoughts, and impulses. If I am numb to my bellyache, I will not be motivated to find ways to feel better. If I ignore my inkling to stop and look both ways before crossing a roadway, I may get hit by a passing vehicle. If I am mentally busy with regrets, like I was when I had committed to painting the boards for the kitchen, I am in a repeating loop of angry feelings and clenched jaw. I had to slow down in order to shift into a softer body, and softer mindset.

Awareness is considered to be the predecessor of change. Awareness plus intention bring our focus to implementing change in a chosen area, at least temporarily eliminating the millions of distractions that keep us from pursuing what we want—and noticing if we're making progress. Most of our changes will be from stuck places to more fluidity, like when I figure out how to soften the brace between me and my horse as I ask him to back up. These stuck places also appear as dissociative moments when attention is far away even while our body is right here. In essence, we are missing in action. Yet it's possible to change the ways we dance with our find/fight/flight/freeze/collapse responses, with our moments of connection, anxiety, defensiveness, depression, and apathy.

When experimenting with creating and following a particular plan like Manley's, I needed to know what he could do, and also believe he could do what I was asking, as I built on his existing skills and knowledge. It's my job to keep track of any horse's responses to my requests. I am assessing competence and looking for calm responsiveness. That's my ideal, and even as I keep that in mind, I want to pay attention to the baby steps of learning what the horse is showing me.

Ram Dass, an American spiritual teacher, said, "We are all affecting the world every moment, whether we mean to or not.

Our actions and states of mind matter, because we are so deeply interconnected with one another." Wanting to be one of those who affects others intentionally—not by accident—motivates me along this journey of awareness through life.

CHAPTER 13

Pressure

What is the value of "yes" if "no" isn't possible?
— Leslie Desmond

The Pushy One

It is very easy for me to push. One might say I'm a natural at pushing. In fact, I was professionally trained to push in politically correct ways—that's part of being a psychotherapist. Mindfully using words to direct the conversation, the introspection, the therapeutic activity, nudging toward those *aha* moments when someone softens into the here and now, and change can seep through the defenses.

My clinical pushiness worked well for the most part, and people seemed grateful for the encouragement to explore, open up, risk, reveal, revel.

With horses, it's a different matter altogether. It's quite black and white—either I'm pushing them to do something that is my idea, or I'm letting them do something that they think is their idea.

So easy to verbalize. So hard to integrate into my life.

Two trail rides, two days in a row, two outcomes. I wish I could say I did better on the second trail ride. But I didn't. Instead, I learned in a bigger way, and I will count that toward "did better."

I had invited my friend Jan to join me for a trail ride after work. We had both been busy, and it'd been months since we'd ridden out together.

I'd been practicing patience with a few students who had come to ride with me, and I offered Jan that same patience while she caught and groomed and tacked up my horse Prince, her horse for this ride. It was not something she'd done often, and although I thought she would benefit from my reminders, I left her to do what she could on her own. She asked for help when she needed it. This all felt really good.

There we were on Rusty and Prince, two horses who could use a little more confidence. I'd already been experimenting with how to help Rusty have enough confidence to carry me out for a trail ride any time I wanted. What had worked was a lot of patience and being persistent with my intention, but without any insistence—that pushiness that comes so easily to me.

Often when I've ridden out on Rusty, we'd go until I felt him hesitating. I'd invite him to stop and check things out, waiting and feeling for those moments of his letting down with a big exhale, lowering his head, and feeling more relaxed. Then I'd ask him to go forward again.

We had many moments like this on our trail ride. Both Rusty and Prince were hesitant, checking out each driveway we came to, especially the one with the mailbox painted with red stripes. Jan and I did well offering our patience to these horses, and we made our way along, finding some areas where all four of us were walking without fear—eager and forward.

For some reason, unknown to us simple-minded humans, our horses worried as much on the way home as heading out. I managed myself through a few moments of impatience and incredulity, and resumed the wait-until-you're-ready approach. Jan had some good learning moments with Prince, which sweetened the ride for me. Then I tried something new, piecing together things I'd seen and tried in the past at clinics.

When Rusty stopped, instead of leaving him stopped, I asked him to move but let him move in any direction. He kept heading away from home, opposite from the direction I thought we should be going and that I thought he would choose. His logic puzzled me.

He walked some steps in his chosen direction and then I picked up a rein and asked for him to change direction, releasing when he was partway into the turn heading us back in the direction I was thinking about.

We did this about nine times. Then on the tenth time, when I asked for movement, he moved forward. Woo-hoo! This felt much better to me than sitting and waiting for him to change his mind.

I think this worked out because Rusty was in that middle level of worry. He could stand still, but still was worried. He let go of his worry a little more smoothly when I invited him to move and let him take us in the direction that felt right to him. I didn't apply pressure or make him work when he made a choice. I just went along for a short while and then asked if he would come back the other way. If he'd been more worried and I'd asked him to stand still, he would have been standing stock still with full-body rigidity. And if I'd asked him to move from that type of standstill, he would likely have gone from rigid to bolting.

So, he was able to listen even though he was not comfortable going with my idea. So we went with his idea, and then I asked again. At some point, obviously, he was able to go with my idea. That change was sweet.

The next day I intended to head out, following the dirt road for a half mile before veering right onto the wooded trail that circled back toward home. I was on Rusty, with a young neighbor Patsy, on Soli, my mellow, older Haflinger. I thought this would be a recipe for success. But no: Rusty was hesitant and Soli was hesitant, and even when Soli went forward, he did not draw Rusty along.

I found myself getting a little frustrated, so I got off and led Rusty. He came as usual although I could feel (and see) his heightened state of alert. "Code Yellow," shall I call it? But even in Code Yellow, Rusty would follow me anywhere when my feet were on the ground.

At some point, I felt ready to mount up again, and decided I would push him, from the saddle, in an experiment to see what happens if I push without frustration or anger, just intention. I paid close attention when I released my push (squeezing legs). Sometimes I accepted his I'm-going-but-I'm-reluctant movement, and sometimes he surprised me with his I'm-curious-and-eager movement.

I learned that pushing doesn't lead to not pushing. Honestly, I tried this a few more times under a few slight variations of trail ride conditions (different trail buddies, different trails, different saddles, different weather), and the results were the same. Pushing does not lead to not pushing, despite my hope that conscious pushing would work.

I also learned that pushing without emotion allowed me to sense when Rusty was shifting from Code Yellow to Code Red. I'm glad I learned to feel this. Pushing in the past led to occasions when seemingly suddenly, Rusty was in Code Red and running for his life.

I've been experimenting more with waiting for Rusty to be ready to move forward. Me managing my urge to push. And all goes well. My main takeaway? I need to be the one to change.

Bracing

We were looking for a new horse to join our herd of therapy horses, and Ruby was a strong candidate for the job. Her first "job interview" with Emma, the horse herd coordinator, went well, and it was time for Ruby's second interview. I was invited to accompany Emma and Fiona, a seasoned instructor, to assess this latest candidate. I felt privileged and included as a newer instructor who brought to this job a head full of opinions about horse training issues. I liked these two colleagues and figured the time together would be worth it, even if we decided against buying this horse we were going to meet at a sales barn a few hours away.

I could tell right away why Ruby was a strong candidate. She was a large pony built like a draft horse. Her combination of short size and broad back fueled our hopes as we pictured her carrying those riders who needed hands-on support from sidewalkers. Ruby was a redhead with big eyes and a long mane and tail. Her good looks guaranteed everyone would fall in love. Buying this mare with an unknown history was an enticing prospect... and a big risk.

Ruby was minimally curious about us newcomers, not surprising for a horse who's been moved to an unfamiliar setting and thrown into a herd of strangers. Horses shut down when life becomes overly confusing and they can't use their primary survival strategy of connecting with a familiar herd, or their options to flee or fight. Eating grass was more important than we were, and this impeded us from exploring what she knew. We found out how she responded to our requests: dragging us to the nearest edibles. That tug-of-war game wasn't fun.

For our therapy lessons, we like when the horse walks when we ask and stops when we ask, turns when we ask and stands still when we ask. Pretty simple. We also need the horse to be comfortable with a balanced rider or an unbalanced rider, with a variety of leaders, a variety of instructors, and one or two or sometimes three volunteers nearby, while standing still, walking, and trotting. The best therapy horse tolerates sudden loud sounds, sudden awkward movements, and beanbags being tossed overhead on purpose, or accidentally between legs or bouncing off backs. We need a horse who is calm and able to stay calm despite a slew of environmental surprises. Ruby's shorter size meant the sidewalkers could support a vulnerable rider without straining their arms and backs and necks while walking along and reaching up at the same time, using their own strength to keep the rider on the horse's back.

As I said, Ruby was pleasant to look at and built well for the job. Otherwise, Ruby did not qualify as a therapy horse. She was what we call a green horse. That's not the color of her hair, but the term describing a horse who knows little of what humans want or how to easily go along with the humans' ideas. She was minimally trained to be easy to handle or ride.

Ruby really wasn't suited for our program's needs. I hinted that she might not be the best for our program. I added that, in order to succeed with us, she would need a lot of retraining as well as training. The retraining would help her respond to pressure by yielding, not pushing with more pressure, which was her habit. It was what she knew. It was what she'd learned. It was what had gotten her through life so far. I experienced this when I got her away from the grass and could lead her. I turned left as we were walking, using the lead rope to draw her nose with me through the turn. In response, she leaned to the right with her nose, her head, her neck, her shoulders, her torso, and her hindquarters. I'm not fond of horses who do this, even though I know that with careful handling, a horse like Ruby could learn to yield to pressure. And more importantly, she could learn to trust and enjoy following a person with or without a halter and lead rope.

The short story? Good looks and heaps of hopes overrode the concerns, and Ruby was purchased. The long story? She was hard to handle for most leaders. She couldn't be used for independent riders, other than instructors like me who invested time in helping her understand what it means to be directed by someone on her back. The end of the story? She injured a staff member while barging through a partially open stall door. That incident was tragic but an excellent example of how dangerous it is for humans when a horse doesn't understand yielding to pressure.

Ruby was rehomed as a companion horse. It's interesting to think what equine treatment plan would have helped her. A challenge for many therapeutic riding programs is providing consistent handling when an amazing array of dedicated volunteers are catching, grooming, tacking, and leading the lesson horses. We would have to be consistent with our requests and our expectations in order to help her respond the way we needed her to respond if she was going to work out as a safe lesson horse. Every staff member and volunteer would need to offer Ruby the same requests and the same responses, first as she was learning what we expected of her, and then to maintain the changes we liked.

Ruby's treatment plan would have addressed how to help her start to trust our guidance and discover that it feels good to let go of bracing and self-protective postures and mindset. She came with a conviction about how to take care of herself around humans, which included wariness and disinterest. Her survival instincts were strong, and she was physically strong and accustomed to pushing through pressure. Teaching her what was expected and reinforcing this instruction through consistent requests could help her become comfortable, allowing another to make decisions for her. Because she was accustomed to tuning out our requests, there would always be the question of whether she could listen to a person or not. Her foundation of distrust meant she was a horse best owned and handled by one person who could offer what a large therapeutic riding program couldn't: consistent attention and expectations.

It's also interesting to think what would have happened if I hadn't cowered in the face of my colleagues, if I'd been pushy enough myself to say, "Bad idea. I'm firmly against the idea of Ruby coming to work with us. She has potential, yes, but we don't have what she needs to get her there. It wouldn't be fair to her or safe for our riders and volunteers to expect her to work out."

Ruby's Treatment Plan

Problems:
1. Pushes into pressure, fails to yield or give way.
2. Disinterested in interacting with people.

Strengths:
1. Steady forward movement.
2. Sturdily built so can balance carrying heavier riders.
3. Even-tempered.

Objectives:
1. Readily yield to pressure in all directions: forward, back, left, right, up, and down while being led.
2. Become curious about interacting with people.

Actions:
1. Backing up to learn softness and engage hindquarters.
2. Frequent transitions (halt/walk/halt) and changes of direction while being led or ridden, to assess her current status regarding yielding of mind and body.
3. Specify and limit who handles and trains with her for a minimum of one month.
4. Introduce activities that elicit her interest, involvement, and problem-solving skills while rewarding her for responsiveness and engaging mentally and emotionally.
5. Offer her a release from pressure during or after any gait or direction transition to encourage doing things without pressure.

Implementation:
1. Who: herd coordinator and specifically identified instructors.
2. How often: 5-7 times a week.
3. Length of each session: ½ hour.
4. For how long until reassessment: 2 weeks.

Assessments:
1. Halt, walk, halt transitions in response to body language or soft directing contact.
2. Left and right turns in response to body language or soft directing contact.
3. Stands and waits at stall doors and pasture gates.

Don't Hurry Me!

Tasia was a feisty, determined little girl taking therapeutic riding lessons—little in terms of both immaturity and her diminutive size. But she was not at all little when it came to expressing herself. Her compromised joints prevented normal rippling movement from her ankles to her jaw as she ambled across the sand in the arena. Her body's stiffness matched her determination to be in charge of something. It felt like she wanted to control us, luring our attention here and there, away from the lesson plan goal of walking independently to the mounting ramp, up the ramp, and, with assistance, mounting Dandy, her lesson horse. I nicknamed her the Petite Queen of Distracting—her mind moved away from the lesson plan faster than her body could.

I had been called in to observe and offer help with this lesson because Tasia's pattern of refusing to follow directions baffled her instructor, Meg. I was intimidated. Who was I to offer guidance to Meg? She was my elder in the field of therapeutic riding, with many more years of experience, and she brought more creativity, enthusiasm, and skills to each student than I could imagine possible. I was asked to intervene because I had the skills from my other jobs as psychotherapist and horse trainer, and I was good at reading and interpreting the unspoken language of the body.

Tasia was delightful even as she provoked her instructor and volunteers each week. She arrived full of unbridled zest and invisible fear, accompanied by a domineering parent. She hated getting on Dandy, despite the bribes being called out from the sidelines from her parent. "Go on, Tasia. Get on Dandy. It's time to ride." Two minutes later, "If you don't get on, we won't stop for ice cream on the way home."

When teaching a child, I make efforts to connect with the parents. I'm comfortable praising the willfulness of their child. Why? Because it means the parents have not subdued the child's natural expressiveness. These traits will later serve the child. Once the child has grown up, we'll admire this willfulness as a strong leadership skill. I have no idea if parents ever listened to me, but I spoke up anyway. I needed to hear myself say that and remind myself to pause and find some curiosity and enjoyment with the children who were comfortable challenging us.

Some parents were intent on having their children follow directions, perform well, and complete tasks. When instructors are expected to prioritize the parents' wishes over the child's needs, conflicts can ensue between parent and child, between parent and instructor, and between instructor and child. After all, parents are the ones who are legally in charge of their child, and often the ones who paid for the lessons. They have the right to determine what's best for their child, and we are careful to honor that they know their child much, much better than we ever will.

There's a problem, though, when the parents themselves are blinded by their own histories and ways of relating. And although I wasn't working there as a family therapist, these particular professional skills were showing up in my thinking about Tasia and her parents. I wanted to understand Tasia's distress and find a way to make things easier for her and her parents. My trauma-informed perspective centered around understanding how our bodies hold on to overwhelming experiences. My observation skills allowed me to envision Tasia's deep fears underlying the willfulness apparent at the start of her riding lessons. That willfulness showed up as a string of indirectly expressed nos.

Before starting her trek to the mounting block, Tasia pointed to a lesson horse being led at the other end of the arena and asked, "What's that horse's name?" Pointing to the rider in that lesson, "Who is that?" Then, "What does Dandy like to eat?" and "Why are those poles on the ground?" These verbal distractions were obvious to me as Tasia fired question after question at anybody who would listen. She was intelligent, and her verbal skills helped her avoid her fear by delaying actually getting on the horse and riding.

The expectation was that Tasia would ride. This is why she came for therapeutic riding lessons. Her parents expected this; the staff expected this. The teaching team hadn't been able to suspend this expectation long enough to appreciate the degree of unreadiness she was showing us in everything she didn't say. From the sidelines where I stood watching, I could see the fear loud and clear. She held her breath and clenched her jaw, and her whole body went rigid each time Meg encouraged her to step close to Dandy in order to mount. And that is what I wanted to address—the messages of Tasia's body language. I wanted to name them and listen to her responses. Name them and intervene on behalf of her fear even if she was unable or unwilling herself to acknowledge fear.

Tasia's denial (*I'm not afraid*) and avoidance (*I'll do anything other than get on Dandy*) were both important survival strategies, designed to distance her from the scary horseback riding while allowing her to stay connected with her parents and instructor by pleasing them.

Week after week, Tasia's reluctance was overridden by her instructor who, well-intentioned but larger and stronger than Tasia, was not unlike her parents. For me, keeping her parents engaged was important, as was helping Tasia through her fearfulness. I wanted Tasia to decide to mount Dandy rather than be lifted and placed there by Meg. I wanted Tasia's parents to watch what I was doing, reevaluate their expectations, and try new things, much like when I train a horse and want the horse's owner involved. Yes, I can make a difference for the child or the horse, but it is the people who are involved for the long run who can make a lasting difference.

I conferred with Meg and got permission to slow things down. Maybe no riding, not even mounting, for a week or two, or until Tasia could let us know she was ready.

I stepped close to Tasia, resting my eyes softly on her. I observed her breathing and checked if her gaze was fixed or shifting as she listened. I noticed other indications that some calm was emerging from her fear as she listened to me: body messages such as eyes blinking, shoulders relaxing, and soft movements of her head and neck. I noticed these changes as I was talking to her using my bedtime-story tone of voice. "Ah, Dandy just turned her head to you. Big head—it's a little scary, isn't it? She's curious about you. Horses like to sniff us. It's part of how they get to know us, how they tell if we are friendly. I'm right here with you, Tasia. If you're scared by her big head, I can help you learn how to stop her from coming close. Put your hands up like this in front of you. There you go. See? Dandy moved her head away."

I supported Tasia's choices and educated her about her fear, her sense of being hurried, and how to protect her sense of safety by using words to set boundaries. Boundaries are a way to manage pressure from others. I advocated that Meg allow her to approach mounting at her own pace—getting ready, step by step, by pausing with a little bit of fear rather than getting flooded by being put on the horse without choice or time to transition.

Pressure

I want to be the one determining how and when I experience pressure. I welcome it when I'm receiving bodywork from someone who negotiates with me just how much pressure I want. Or when I'm wearing my favorite tights for an exercise class. Or when I'm tucked under the covers with a hot water bottle resting on my abdomen. Otherwise, I don't like pressure. Even though the pressure of a deadline helps me harvest the ripe blueberries and file my tax return.

Our nervous systems might respond to pressure with aliveness through sympathetic activation, or with calmness through parasympathetic activation. When pressure is released, either one or both in combination can occur. Imagine being embraced by someone you love and feel safe with. That pressure would elicit a parasympathetic response, melting into the comfort of this contact. Imagine that even if it's by someone you love, you are being hugged a bit longer or tighter than you want right then. Sympathetic activation appears as the desire to get away from the hug, which might progress to you saying out loud, "Hey, lighten up a bit." Or silently feeling smothered, helpless, and resentful. With Tasia, her flight response was triggered by the pressure of lesson expectations, and her flight pattern took her (and her teaching team) into conversational distractions that helped her avoid the discomfort of having a flight urge that she couldn't act on.

Our horses can have a similar mix of responses. In some ways, we're confining them in a hug whether they like it or not, because we contain them with our fences and other lifestyle choices. As their captors and teachers, it's our responsibility to pay attention and adjust pressure whenever we can. We want their environments—including relationships with us—to be more comforting than threatening. We want to help them understand what we want, not trigger their urge to get away from us.

I was taught in my first riding lessons with the Moffats that offering a release from pressure was a reward. Instead of patting my horse when he did something well, I sat quietly. Thirty years later, I heard something similar from an assortment of horsemanship clinicians who said *this is what I wanted* by releasing pressure once the horse responded, like loosening the reins or stopping leg pressure. It is a valid training approach, although not the only one we can use.

Another application of release is offering it as an invitation, a low- or no-pressure space for horses to learn to anticipate and choose. I remember walking on a crowded sidewalk in Manhattan and using my peripheral vision to notice where there were openings between people as we were moving, and heading for those to avoid bumping into anyone. Another way to conceptualize this is to offer the release before the pressure, not afterwards. Offering a way out before we ask the horses to tolerate confinement, like teaching them how to get out of a trailer before we expect them to stay in one. Or helping Tasia avoid riding until she knew she was in charge of deciding if and when she would ride.

A release can be the actual lessening of contact, by putting slack in the reins for example, or it can be the intention and energy of communicating yes without actually changing the amount of pressure in the contact. Horsemanship clinician Mark Rashid introduced me to the latter, and I explored it further while practicing Aikido. (It sounds a little woo-woo, and if I could describe this better, I would.)

Unless pressure is meaningful to the horse, it adds confusion. The release needs to be as meaningful as the pressure that precedes it. I used to talk with my hands while holding a lead rope, signaling nonsense to my horse while I was busy chatting with friends. Those moments of accidental pressure and release teach our horses that we're confusing and inconsistent and therefore scary. Whatever the case, they want to get away from the nonsensical, and will do so by physically moving away, or, if they can't do that, by mentally leaving.

If the horse doesn't know how to reduce or end the pressure, it will feel trapped, and as with the too-tight hug, the horse's sympathetic flight/fight instincts are stimulated. The horse needs to know how to get release from pressure. These horse instincts mean we have to present our ideas to them so that they can learn how to co-create this reduced pressure. The concept is quite simple. What isn't so simple is retraining our human minds and bodies. I suspect it would be an easier path for people very new to horses than it is for folks like me. They have no old habits to replace.

Some say with horses, the release into zero pressure is the teacher of yes. With our horses living in captivity, however, I'm not convinced we ever offer them zero pressure. Instead, they can learn to search for less pressure when we're handling them. It falls on us to know when we are pressuring the horse and when we are releasing the pressure, and notice how the horse is responding. We must also do this consistently and intentionally. These practices are how we could have helped Ruby.

Harry Whitney said, "Never add pressure to a disturbed horse." I came to understand this in the Somatic Experiencing® training. I learned about sympathetic and parasympathetic activation, discharge, and settling cycles, and started noticing how my own ability to take in new information varied. I could be alert and learning, alert and looking for an excuse to leave the classroom, or sleepy and missing the intellectual aspects of what was being presented. I needed the right balance of sympathetic and parasympathetic activation to be learning. Too much sympathetic? I couldn't learn because I was scheming how to get away or daydreaming of being elsewhere. Remember being an elementary school student where your job was to sit, focus on the teacher, be ready to answer questions, and sit, sit, sit? It felt especially torturous when your preference was to be romping through the woods and fields or snuggling into an armchair with a horse story or a *Nancy Drew* mystery.

We can't expect our horses to respond to pressure when they are bothered by anything in their environment, whether it's from our doing or from elsewhere. As with Rusty, a little bit of pressure could send him into a panic when he was already harboring worry. Like the proverbial straw that breaks a camel's back. He taught me he can't learn when there's too much pressure. And he taught me to notice his subtle signs of being worried. We can't expect ourselves to learn under pressure, either.

CHAPTER 14

Falls and Co-regulation

*Trauma is not what happens to us, but what we hold
inside in the absence of an empathetic witness.*
— GABOR MATÉ

Getting Together with Rusty

R USTY AND I were in the round pen after the fact—after I fell off him while riding in the arena. I had not realized how much we were not together mentally... until we were not together physically either. He had turned and sped up suddenly, and I hadn't gone with him. I hadn't been present and feeling his readiness to change direction and speed. I landed on my side. Ouch. Then and there I vowed to do more in the round pen—with the goal of developing a stronger connection with him—before I mounted.

Rusty offered obedience without much asking on my part. However, I wanted something else, something more. I wanted his willing attention, his curiosity, his readiness to join me mentally and physically.

I went at a snail's pace that day to please my still aching body. I gave Rusty (and myself) frequent pauses, communicating "breaktime" with my body language and energy level by coming to a full stop, looking away, and relaxing whatever body parts weren't needed for standing upright. Things were going well. He didn't do much. I didn't do much. But mentally he was alert, and emotionally he was softening—his head was dropping lower, his eyes were blinking, and he had long sequences of yawning. As if he'd been waiting for me to offer this degree of slow.

I'd been wanting Rusty to stay with me mentally, and I became curious if I could stay with him mentally. I lost the feel of togetherness when I was walking between him and the fence panels, too close to the panels for comfort. As soon as I thought, "I could get squished," his head flew up and he stopped. I stopped. What had just happened? Was it something I did? I'd had this thought that created fear in me and it reverberated to him. We disconnected. I think he was expecting trouble from me because I've blamed him for my fear many times, unconscious of how my upset troubled him. He feels my upset but cannot understand it, and it worries him. I stood for a few minutes allowing myself to settle, noticing Rusty's calm returning.

I felt better after our time in the round pen. Although my body still hurt from the fall, I felt confident that I could build this sense of togetherness with Rusty that makes all we do so satisfying. And I could regain our connection after I broke it. He is a dear horse and I owe it to him to figure out what ties me up inside. I had the sense he was letting go of his own deep-inside worried places, which I blame myself for. Too many times in the past I confronted him with too much emotion and too little guidance.

The road of life is always under construction. Someone else said that. The journey of conscious horsemanship is continuously stimulating. I say that.

Self-Propelled

There are many ways to come off a horse.

Tricia came for therapeutic lessons in the milder New England seasons of spring, summer, and fall, and seemed most to enjoy surprising us. She kept us on alert every lesson once she discovered she could launch herself without warning from Candy, the robust black and white pony she rode. Tricia was an older teen, slight in build, but compact and physically strong enough to exert some oomph in her self-determined efforts to dismount.

We were seldom sure if Tricia understood language any better than she expressed it, but we got better at noticing her body language and what happened before she started to get down from her horse—the look in her eyes as she glanced at the volunteers, the hint of a grin forming, the start of her leaning to one side. This was the best time to intervene. Once set in motion, the fall became a dance of directing her body to a safe landing. The volunteers excelled at averting her from colliding with the ground. Sometimes crocodile tears formed in Tricia's eyes when she was prevented from dismounting. Was this her effort to make the volunteers feel guilty for interrupting her play?

Tricia's prior instructors had asked the volunteers to keep her on the horse, to prevent her from dismounting in the middle of a lesson. This had created a gentle battle—enjoyable for her, but not so enjoyable for the volunteers.

The safety of the volunteers was as much my responsibility as the safety of the rider, so I decided to experiment. What would happen if we allowed Tricia to dismount, assisted by the sidewalkers for safety, then asked her to lead Candy back to the mounting ramp where she would get on again? We knew she wasn't fond of walking and had seen her fear amplified when she was walking with a large animal close by. She stayed as far from Candy as she could, holding the end of the lead rope, head turned to watch where Candy was rather than watching where she was going. We worried as we watched and stayed close in case we needed to intervene.

Something must have clicked for Tricia. The number of sudden dismounts started diminishing as she engaged in other aspects of the lessons, such as holding the reins or tossing and catching a beanbag with the volunteers.

I also explored what other riding activities might interest her in staying on Candy so that we could avoid the dismounting skirmishes altogether. Trotting. Her enjoyment of sitting on a trotting horse was more captivating than her game of sudden dismount. I learned much about how I had underestimated her.

Will You Catch Me?

Another rider, younger and smaller than Tricia, had a different relationship to dismounting. Marty was scared. She distracted us at the end of each lesson with questions and random comments, until I realized she was avoiding dismounting. She was scared to cover the distance between sitting on the back of her horse Stan, and standing with her own two feet on the ground. I suspected Marty needed to know we would help her bridge that gap and would also catch her if she lost her balance while riding, so I incorporated this into her lesson plan. She would mount Stan and then orient and settle by looking for the familiar small plastic horses placed around the ring while she and Stan were being led. Then she would practice falling off and being caught by the volunteers.

Marty liked to ride lying back on Stan as part of her lesson. This was a great position for dismounting practice. While the volunteer leader directed Stan, I walked close on one side, and the volunteer sidewalker walked on the other side. Both of us were alert and in place to catch Marty.

We talked in advance about the plan: Marty would lie back on Stan, then look at us when she was ready to slide into our arms. She would let herself lose her balance, and we would catch her. She followed this plan sometimes, and other times she skipped the letting-us-know-she-was-ready part of the plan. We caught her every time anyway.

She progressed from sliding into our arms with eyes wide open and breath held, to sliding with eyes closed and breath held. She was surprised each time we caught her, surprised that we didn't disappear at the last minute. As she started to trust, a gentle quality accompanied her falling. It made me wonder if being caught and protected from falling to the ground had been more shocking than her expectation that we would not notice her falling, would not keep her from hitting the ground hard.

First Aid for Falls

1. Prioritize attending to your own responses until you are relatively calm.
2. Keep the rider still, quiet, and warm.
3. Reassure the rider that the horse is fine and is with (name the person who is handling the horse).
4. Encourage plenty of time for safety, rest, and orienting.
5. Offer comforting physical contact in a nonrestrictive way, like a hand on the rider's arm, whenever appropriate.
6. Gently inquire about sensations as the rider's shock wears off, asking about the internal experience: What are you noticing in your body?
7. Allow a full minute or two of silence between questions, watching for body language signs of activation and settling.
8. Encourage the rider to rest more before talking about the fall.
9. Continue to listen for and validate the rider's physical responses.
10. Pay attention to the rider's emotional responses.

Falls and Co-regulation

I've had my share of falls from horses, haystacks, even ladders. There's nothing safe about falls unless you're a toddler on a padded floor or an experienced Aikidoist. I've assisted others as they recover balance and confidence, drawing on my professional skills from Somatic Experiencing® (SE™) and Bodywork and Somatic Education™ (BASE™) trainings and practice, and my personal healing experiences. I've wanted to bring to the therapeutic riding profession an expanded understanding of how to respond to people after a fall. Helping a rider's nervous system reset, right then and there, goes hand in hand with checking for concussions and broken bones.

I have also explored aspects of recovering confidence and trust—in oneself as well as in the horse—when ready to ride again. Even though horse people may seek help weeks or months or years after a bad fall, there's always hope for healing body and spirit, balance and confidence, no matter how long it's been since the fall.

I enjoy helping people feel more themselves, more ready to get involved with activities they love. People who are troubled by fear or disorientation from a prior fall may feel cautious or uncertain about resuming horse activities, may lose balance more often than before, may simply be wondering if prior falls and accidents are still affecting them.

Physiologically we are overwhelmed when we fall. We lose balance and lose control, and the impact of body against hard surface happens too fast for us to process and leaves us injured. We are instantaneously trying to orient and protect ourselves, faster than our thoughts can track. We don't have time to even notice these orientation and defensive responses.

These incomplete, thwarted responses are the problem. They live on in our bodies until we give them time and attention to be felt and allowed to settle. The calm presence of another person is a key element for feeling safe and starting to resolve those extremely scary experiences from the past. I think Marty's need to be caught came from her history of deficits when nobody had been there to attune to her emotions, nor support her early physical efforts to stand and walk. Tricia, on the other hand, seemed to have no qualms about falling off her horse.

As helpers, the more we become familiar with our own nervous systems and past fear responses, the more we can identify, assess, and help others allow their stuck survival responses to surface. This ability applies to our helping humans and horses.

Co-regulation is our innate capacity for relying on calmer people to help us feel safe while we settle after an upset. We are hardwired for this reliance, whether with animals or people. We also will co-regulate with others who are in a distressed state, unless we know how to connect with our own place of calm even in the middle of others' energetic storms.

Nobody is born with self-regulation. It starts to develop in early childhood and in the presence of those who have developed self-regulation. The fetus, newborn, and infant are fully reliant on the regulating capacities of others. The fetus shares the mother's physiology. The newborn shares the nervous system of the caregiver. Nobody that young has any ability to set boundaries or act independently for wellness or self-protection.

When there's worry and conflict in my human relationships, I sometimes ask myself, "Who's going to be the adult here? Who will shift into a more mindful state, pause the acting out of upset thoughts and feelings, and allow the other's waves of upset to crest, break, and settle?"

When it comes to relating with a horse, I do not ask who is going to be the adult, me or the horse. The adult with a regulated nervous system—that has to be me, as much as I would love to feel all those warm fuzzy feelings if I let myself be a needy child, with my horse as the regulator. That would end in disappointment, if not injury. Injury for me. It's our human job—not the horse's—to be calm and present and help the horse join us in this state.

It took me a while to recognize that my being upset caused Rusty to be upset. It helped us both to feel safe together when I took care of settling myself before doing anything with him.

Sometimes, we need to wait as the horse has its horse experiences, waiting without getting upset, angry, or afraid when the horse is dysregulated. When the horse is calm again, it is easier to feel safe together. When we feel safe together, we can proceed with plans based on what we know the horse understands and can perform, physically and emotionally. This is what I call cooperation. And we humans hold the key to eliciting this cooperation from our horses.

The role of the calm adult is to evoke the down-regulation of another's autonomic nervous system. When I am the calm adult, I first take care of my own needs to settle, doing whatever I can to access my sense of feeling safe and grounded. Then I can be present for others to do the same. After a fall with no major injury, this means guiding the fallen person to pause long enough to orient to the idea *I am safe now.* Safe environment, safe person, safe body. Give the fallen person permission and emotionally neutral support to allow the normal body responses to occur (trembling, tears, shaking it off, yawning, seeking safety and quiet) while the adrenaline response completes and discharges, like the waves of activation crest, break, and settle.

We have to guess when we are supporting those who don't have words for what they are experiencing or needing. Our guesses are based somewhat on knowledge and somewhat on our primal urges to foster connection.

Touch can be supportive after a fall. When I am going to offer touch, I keep my intentions clear, even if I never say them out loud: I'm letting you know I am here, and you are not alone. My intention is to share my calm okayness with you, and help you reconnect with your own grounded wholeness. I am here with you as a calm adult in charge so you can settle and restore at your own pace. My intention is to support your own healing wisdom so you can allow your body to sense and release anything leftover, as you start to come into a more embodied presence. My intention is to support you without my own fears interrupting your process.

And, I will ask permission before I touch you.

Part Four:
Especially This

CHAPTER 15

Transitions

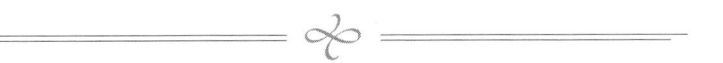

We bereaved are not alone. We belong to the largest company in all the world—the company of those who have known suffering. — HELEN KELLER

THAT SATURDAY

"ONE, TWO, THREE, PULL!" Rusty was cast again, stuck lying down in the wrong position, feet jammed against the wall, unable to get up on his own—similar to when he was six months old. We needed to move him, to change his position.

Terry had found Rusty this way in the run-in shed and yelled to me, "Rusty has passed!" Eyes widening in the beginnings of shock, but still with some hope that it wasn't true, I started toward the shed. Images flooded me from two separate occasions when we had found beloved horses dying when we went out for morning chores. I was stunned.

I looked to where Terry stood, noticed his horse Sam standing next to him, then made out an awkward dark mass in the shadows of the shed. Rusty was down, on the ground, at a time when he shouldn't be. "What?"

Terry yelled again, "Rusty is cast. He's *cast!*"

Rusty wasn't dead. This sank in enough to get me running—Rusty was alive! As I got close, I saw him lying upside down, eyes rolling, groaning, head extended and teeth gnawing at the shed wall—little else in motion. I was horrified. I didn't know how long he'd been stuck lying this way, and it was a life-threatening situation—horses have trouble breathing if they are down too long. Plus this was the second time Rusty was cast, and my terror from twenty-four years prior popped up in full force.

Despite all this, I moved into action. I told Rusty, "We're going to help you. I'll be right back," then sprinted to the tack room, grabbed a couple of long ropes, and sprinted back.

Together Terry and I looped the ropes around Rusty's legs, stepped back, and rocked his body, turning him over, away from the wall. We stood back out of the way as he got to his feet, took a big breath, then ambled over to a pile of hay and started eating.

I sank to my knees. My heart rate was off the charts from sprinting, from the effort to roll him over, from the adrenaline rush of angst that came when I thought Rusty might have been cast for long enough to be dying.

I crouched there, leaning on one arm while pressing on my pounding heart with my free hand. I was breathing hard at maximum imaginable capacity, and letting my body make sounds that matched my fear and exertion and relief.

Terry came to stand beside me and put his hand on my shoulder, asking if I was okay. I leaned into our contact. I was okay. At least I was pretty sure I was okay, although my pounding heart worried me. I kept pressing on it with my hand.

As things started to settle, I wrapped my arms around myself and let my curiosity grow about this arousal and settling process. I could breathe easily again, and my heart rate was slowing down. Rusty appeared as if nothing had happened, not dull or disoriented from being in shock, nor unsteady on his feet. He was okay. I was okay. We all were okay.

Except Terry's horse Sam. He had been alarmed by my dash to the shed with ropes flopping in my arms. He was still running back and forth along the fence line, stuck in a fear response triggered by my unusual movement and sounds.

I got up, walked to where he could see me, and spoke to him in my more familiar calm tone of voice. He came to a stop, eyes still wide, before lowering his head and stepping in to sniff my offered hand. He took a deep breath, exhaling much of his tension. Now Sam was okay, too.

Terry came close to hang out with Sam while I hung out with more of my settling process. Rusty was still eating the hay.

I marveled that I hadn't collapsed, even though part of me had gone into shock with that first thought that Rusty was dead. Also remarkable was how intense my physiology became, how easily I could be with it, and how quickly things started to settle after such a huge arousal.

Many times that day I thought back to what had happened. I felt relieved that Terry and I were able to move Rusty's thousand-pound body. I was puzzled that Rusty acted normal right away, with no signs of the physiological collapse that can happen when a horse (or any mammal) is stuck—unable to flee or fight in order to survive—and slips into the immobility of shock. I worried that his apparently normal behavior was covering some internal injuries.

Memories of Terry's physical assistance and emotional support brought tears. I hadn't been alone in this crisis.

I had several episodes of feeling inundated by waves of heartache. This situation reminded me of how helpless we can feel when a beloved is in trouble, even as we take action to save them. This situation reminded me of how vulnerable horses are, even though they are big and powerful, adaptable and resilient in their own horsey ways. This situation reminded me of those near-death experiences early in life when I had been stuck, unable to flee or fight, unaided and feeling alone, and had gone into the immobility of shock.

I love this horse deeply. My heart spreads wide with warmth when I think of Rusty and our twenty-five years together. My heart is heavy with sorrow when I imagine life without him.

That evening, while Rusty was eating, I brought my attention with heightened awareness to smelling him, touching him, listening to his chewing, feeling his warmth, his breathing, his winter coat, his muscles and bones—being with and being touched by the dimensions of his special Rusty-ness.

Although we can't capture these moments as easily as taking a photograph with a camera, I do have this rich blend of memories—sensory and visual, kinesthetic and energetic. And these are mine forever.

With This Chemo

"So, with this chemo, does it mean you've had a diagnosis of liver cancer?"

I was on a videocall with Carly, a vivacious young woman I'd met when she was volunteering in my therapeutic riding lessons. She had texted asking me to call—a rare request. With that ask, I knew she probably had some very important news. We texted a bit more and that's where she had typed "TACE," and I looked up this treatment online.

"Yes," she said, pausing. "Well, actually, I got this diagnosis a year and a half ago. They told me then I had four to six months left and that I should get my affairs in order as soon as possible."

A deep sense of impending loss set in, along with some giddiness hearing that Carly had already outlived the predictions. I scrolled back through my recent memories to when we had last seen each other in person before I'd moved out of state.

Being me, I asked why she hadn't told me sooner. There was a long pause with some barely hidden internal squirming. "I didn't want you to feel sad."

I suspected, and may have even said aloud, that maybe she herself didn't want to feel sad by naming and sharing this news with me. Talking about it would make it real. Perhaps not telling me sooner gave her space to be her "normal" pre-diagnosis self when we'd spent time together. Or, perhaps her reasons were much more complicated and elusive than that.

Carly quickly tired, and we agreed it was naptime for her. But first I shared my memory of having chemotherapy twenty-four years ago as part of the treatment recommended after my breast cancer diagnosis and surgery. I had lost steam every day, suddenly and completely, often and frequently, and too damned much of the time. An exhaustion in every cell that had no wiggle room for being overridden. An exhaustion that I recovered from. A cancer experience that led me to wanting more contact with horses again.

We ended our call and I sat for a minute, letting this sink in a bit more. News like this doesn't sink in all at once. It would take its time, little by little, dropping shock waves randomly through the days to follow. Last-ditch chemo with home nursing care provided by the local hospice agency. And according to her, she won't try any more treatments. Done.

I headed outside, seeking comfort in the form of a hug from Terry after hesitating in the kitchen where I thought about eating, which is another kind of comfort. I needed the hug comfort. And I knew this was available from him. I relaxed into our embrace, gently crying, telling him about the call and my sorrow as we stood in the garden next to the raised bed we had earlier stripped of its dying pea plants.

While I was talking with Carly, Terry had been preparing this bed for its next planting. We were in Virginia where the growing season was long enough to warrant three or four plantings. The bed had been filled with a truckload of local topsoil and planted before we realized it would need help to mitigate the large percentage of clay. The peas grew, despite this soil that preferred to harden rather than crumble, and despite our planting a bit late in the year for their liking.

I was overcome by the need to do something to release these large waves of Death-Is-In-My-Face energy. And there, ready and waiting as I stepped apart from our embrace, was the three-tined cultivating fork. I put both hands on it and started stabbing into the hardened soil surface, prodding and twisting to loosen it and make it ready for our next planting. I was grunting and groaning and exclaiming how much I needed to do this. A most satisfying effort.

And then I was done. Those waves had passed through me into the ground, engaging my attention and many muscles and my cardiovascular system and all that fresh air—all for the visible purpose of readying this garden bed for more seeds. Seeds which would become more plants. Which would feed our bodies eventually. And feed our souls every step of the way.

I remember attacking dandelions one year with similar gusto. Decades before, Linda Molsen, Rusty's breeder, had hit that invisible milestone of no return, when the scales were tipped and cancer had done much more than alarm her immune system. It had taken root and taken over, like the weeds in my lawn, leaving no room for the vegetables or flowers to compete and complete their intended life cycles.

That year, the dandelions were popping up everywhere in my lawn and I was determined to uproot each and every one of them. I dug and I dug and I dug, dislodging dandelion after dandelion after dandelion. About the time I remembered dandelions are edible and have medicinal qualities, I realized that all the dandelion removal I was doing would not keep death away from Linda.

That was then and this was now, and I still felt helpless to change the course of a friend's life. I loved Carly. I loved her spunk and her grit and her laughing in the face of horrors survived. I loved her kindness, her creativity, her vulnerability.

I hated cancer and the hope it was stealing.

Sudden Loss

Brad was a Belgian draft horse. Standing at over sixteen hands high, he was the biggest horse in the therapeutic riding program. His size allowed him to carry the most unbalanced adult riders. Sitting on his broad back was like relaxing on a sturdy, padded rocking chair. His height was a challenge for some riders. Getting on from the mounting ramp was easy. But when it was time to get off, it was scary just looking down and orienting to the distance between up there on his back and down there where the ground waited. Most riders needed emotional support and physical assistance to land safely on the ground. He was a favorite, nonetheless.

I was on the road one morning, headed to town to run some errands before starting my day of lessons at the farm where Brad lived and worked. My route took me past the therapeutic riding center and, as always, I glanced over to see the horses grazing in the fields before their work day started. Like I said before, as far back as I can remember, I've had this habit of keeping track of where horses lived, whether I knew them or not.

Two minutes later my cell phone rang. When I saw who was calling, I pulled off the road to answer it.

"Hi, Robin. What's up?" It was the horse herd coordinator, and I expected she would update me with changes about what horses would be available for my riders.

"Brad is gone. He just passed."

I went still. My attention narrowed to the pounding of my heart and the buzzing in my ears while I waited to breathe. "Oh my god."

Robin filled me in, sounding as stunned as I felt. "He was just lying there. The volunteers went to bring him and Red in. And Brad was lying there on his side as if he was napping. But he didn't get up." I was imagining the scene as I listened. This beloved big horse lying there motionless, lifeless. And the volunteers' shock. Those poor volunteers. Finding a horse dead is not one of the job expectations. Not on a normal, sunny morning. "No sign of thrashing." Robin's voice interrupted my thoughts. "Probably a heart attack. I called the vet already." She paused. "Everybody is upset." And now I was upset, too.

"I'll be there soon, Robin. I'll help figure out how we'll get through today."

Brad was so many special things to so many people. Well-loved by riders and volunteers and instructors as well. He was big and calm, soft and willing to be touched, easily guided when we were leading or riding him. This big horse had been trained to walk, trot, and canter with a rider. He would stand patiently for as long as it took while some of our most physically challenged riders were wheeled or carried up the mounting ramp and carefully placed onto his broad back. Brad seemed content. Content to stand still. Content to walk. Content to trot, but always happy to slow down, like he had a built-in readiness to stop and wait. A horse who would be impossible to replace. There was no other horse that big and broad, no horse that calm and tolerant of human affection, no horse that well trained, no horse that comfortable with an ever-changing series of volunteer handlers, challenging riders, and sidewalkers hanging on his sides as they supported unstable riders high up on Brad's back.

He had been healthy and well and working his usual big draft horse magic in lessons—and then he was dead. I can still feel it in my heart as I think about him. My love, my ache, my mouth-dropping moment of shock when I heard the news. Staff, volunteers, and riders and their families all felt this loss.

Transitions

In the world of equitation—the art and practice of riding horses—the word "transitions" brings images of horses changing from one speed to another. An instructor calls out across the riding arena, "Nice transition, but next time breathe when you're asking your horse to canter." Transitions on horseback can be smooth, choppy, abrupt, hurried, or late.

For everybody else, transitions mark anything that starts, changes, or ends—like starting school, taking a new job, moving into a new relationship or home. These, too, can be smooth or otherwise. We pass through an infinite number of changes from the biggest transitions—birth and death—to those as simple as lying down for a night's sleep and getting up the next day. These are measured by our emotional responses—the bigger the change, the more poignant the memories of gains and losses.

My love for teaching therapeutic riding had become clouded by losses. Instructors moved on to other professions or retired. Volunteers stopped coming because they found paid jobs after months of searching or became ill like Carly. Riders moved away or started lessons in regular programs when they no longer needed the support of the therapeutic team. Horses who were burned out were sold or given away to new homes where they would be free from the stress of adjusting to multiple handlers and riders.

These losses were predictable, yet feelings came like a tidal surge at the full moon. Waves of grief washed through us—staff and volunteers—but seldom overwhelmed us. We knew about these changes in advance and could adjust to them over time. Nonetheless, working as a team to provide therapeutic riding services, we collectively experienced these losses.

Some losses were sudden, like Brad's death, electrifying everyone like a bolt of lightning. Nobody could be prepared. It fell to us staff to support our team members even though we, too, were reeling. Comforting others might have been easier than pausing to feel that rock in the belly, the ache in the heart, the pressure behind the eyes wanting to overflow into tears. But we also had regular activities and responsibilities to fulfill, like lessons to plan and teach, prospective riders to orient, horses to feed. What is the cost when overriding our own needs in order to focus on others?

How do we cope with surprise endings, like the sudden death of a horse, a rider, a rider's parent, a friend? Do we have a community to reach out to? To find solace with? People who share the grief? Do we have rituals that encourage speaking, singing, artwork, movement, or prayer to honor the lives lost? When shock accompanies loss, the support of a calm, regulated person helps us navigate into a life changed by grief. Although we didn't lose Rusty when he was cast, the threat of death had rattled me, and I'd needed Terry's soothing presence.

We depend on others for calming and survival. At the start of life, humans are more vulnerable than horses. Although horses can get up and run the day they are born, we can't. We require others to move us, feed us, and keep us warm and dry. We also need eye contact, touch, and welcome from others of our species.

It's a tragic loss to lose touch with our need for safety and belonging, that nonverbal knowing that I am safe in your presence. We humans can be so wounded we seldom rest deeply and restoratively when we're close to another. A horse who can't rest in the presence of other horses will not survive in the wild. Despite our best intentions, the choices we make as their owners—shelter, space, food, companions—don't always match their needs as horses. Their nature is unchanged despite domestication. They still need the company of their horse buddies for there to be a sense of safety.

How do we honor transitions? Would we notify riders and their families before their next lesson with Brad? Should we have a memorial service for him, inviting all who knew him to come together to share our loving memories, share our sorrow, say our goodbyes? In twenty years as a therapeutic riding instructor, I've been to one celebration of life for a therapy horse who died. The horses were included in that gathering and roamed freely amongst our circle of humans. I like to think other programs do this, but is it the norm? Are transitions and losses adequately addressed, or left in the realm of *If we don't name it, maybe it won't hurt so much?*

Healing from my own trauma and helping others heal from theirs (in my role as psychotherapist), gained priority over helping horses and humans as a therapeutic riding instructor. I continued offering to train volunteers, knowing it would benefit the horses. And even though my office-based work has been fulfilling, I have missed being in the ring with a team of volunteers, a well-trained horse, and a riding student.

Improving how we show up in a relationship demands a different type of transition, an internal shift. We look within and befriend what we find. We grieve and let go when we are ready, leaving space for the new to take root. Committing to a conscious relationship is the hardest thing most of us ever do.

Although my journey with horses and therapeutic riding has not ended, some aspects of it have. One therapeutic riding program moved across town and expanded. Another dissolved after a change in leadership. A third program consolidated from lessons at two leased locations to one program at its own facility. Every horse I knew when I was teaching has gone to a retirement home or died.

Transitions are about moving toward, not just about leaving. Arrivals and departures. Births and deaths. Beginnings and endings. Following every ending is another beginning, tinged with remnants of what ended, and hopes for what will come.

CHAPTER 16

Listening

The greatest show of respect comes from removing your agenda from the picture and listening to what your horse needs instead. He will do anything you ask him to do, as long as you show him that his comfort and self-preservation are your top priority. — GAIL IVEY

SHARING DECISIONS

I WAS ENJOYING A week off from my social work job in community mental health. The weather was perfect for some horse time so I decided to see what I could figure out about Rusty's lack of enthusiasm about being ridden. He was easy to approach in the paddock behind the barn. I haltered and led him into the barn, where he stood calmly munching hay while I groomed and saddled him. He left his hay without a complaint to come with me to the riding ring.

When we arrived at the ring, I realized I hadn't changed into my riding boots, so I removed his halter and left him there while I went for the boots. When I returned, he was standing right where I'd left him.

I'd been thinking about how Rusty accepts the bit after first expressing his no by holding his breath, raising his head above my reach, then lowering his head to the ground. I decided I'd skip the hassle of bridling him—much of which was an annoying puzzle to me—and ride him in his halter. This aligned with my intention to trust him more, trusting what he offers me, trusting I could stay on him if he got worried and jumped around, and trusting that maybe he wouldn't feel the need to get that worried anyway.

As I approached him with halter in hand, he turned and walked off a few steps. Did he think I had the bridle? Could I skip even the halter for this ride in the ring today? Yes, that was a risk I was willing to take. I would ride Rusty with nothing on his head. I laid his halter over the top fence board and placed my hand under his chin, inviting him to come with me to the mounting block. He came right along, lined up alongside the block, and stood still while I mounted. Then he walked off toward the far gate, came to a stop with his head over the gate, and stood there.

I did nothing to intervene. I had already decided this was *his* ride, and I would let him make as many decisions as I could tolerate. It had crossed my mind that his general lack of enthusiasm was in response to my behavior. It had been so easy to direct him, I'd slipped into over-directing him, micromanaging him. To him this probably felt like he didn't have much of a say about what we were doing. We all know that it gets old pretty quickly when we spend time with someone who's running the show all the time.

Rusty stood there for about five minutes. I felt his breath gently billowing under me. I watched where he was looking. I breathed and waited. And then I didn't want to wait any more, so I made a tiny wiggle movement with my left leg to see what would happen. He shifted his weight, and took a step back from the gate. Then he stepped forward and stopped with his head over the gate again. From where I sat, I could see a bit of his facial expression as well as feel his body. He felt at ease. I paused before wiggling my leg again. He stepped off away from my wiggling and walked away from the gate, stopping after about ten steps.

We stood there for about fifteen minutes. Again, I was feeling his breathing and watching what I could of his expression when his head was tilted enough to see his face. Then I felt him take some bigger breaths and sigh, then loosen his jaw with a chewing motion. I wondered if he had been waiting for me to tell him to do something, go someplace, move. But I hadn't.

As Rusty relaxed even more, he cocked his right hind leg, which put me off balance a little. I played around with leaning into the imbalance in slow motion, trusting I wouldn't tip him over. I leaned a little, leaned a little more, then I felt him start to adjust under me. Together with him, I came upright and balanced as he did. More licking and chewing, softening his jaw. Then he cocked that foot again. Again, I leaned in slow motion and waited for him to shift and return me to upright and balanced. He did this a few more times, and then cocked his left hind foot. Same response from me. Then right hind, twice, and a step forward, and all four feet under him—head relaxed, breathing regular, but somehow feeling a little different. Maybe feeling like he was allowing his awareness to include my presence in a different way? Less blocking or tension or something. I don't really know which words would describe it, but it felt better.

I needed to switch gears and get ready to go out to the weekly square dance lesson, so I hopped off and thanked him. I paused, watching his breathing and facial expressions, before I walked off toward the gate closest to the barn. Rusty came along with me and accepted being haltered. I led him back to the barn, where I untacked him and released him out the barn door to the paddock where his herd mates were waiting.

I wanted more confidence in reading his facial expressions. The nostrils, the mouth, the chin, the multitude of wrinkles and movement around the eyes. It was probably enough to know that he was either feeling okay inside himself, or he wasn't. But I wanted more, anything that could help me do more to help him feel better. I hoped I added a little that day to his feeling better in my presence.

My Nay Vote

Most horses need dental work. It helps them move their jaws efficiently and chew without discomfort. Often a trained equine dental professional does the maintenance work called floating—filing smooth those teeth with sharp edges caused by the horse's chewing action.

Harold was the equine dentist I chose to come each year to check if my horses' teeth needed floating. He was a graceful man, ready with a smile, and committed to working without using sedation, a speculum to hold the horse's mouth open, or power tools. He relied on cooperation. Most of my horses liked this about him and cooperated.

I say "most of my horses" because over a stretch of a few visits, Rusty would not let Harold do his job. Rusty's resistance worried me, and I was ready to say, "That's it. Don't bother trying with Rusty anymore." I was a protective owner, probably overprotective. I got upset when I saw Rusty upset. Maybe it was my anxiety that triggered Rusty, not anything about Harold.

And maybe I expected too little from Rusty and allowed him to make too many decisions.

Rusty had been provoking my learning since I'd purchased him as a yearling. I was grateful for the sense (or nonsense?) that led me down this path of horsemanship so he and I could eventually enjoy our time together. I spent our first few years criticizing him and misunderstanding his needs and his communications. I finally learned enough so that some of our time together was indeed *together*. What a relief.

So, when Rusty was not cooperating—tossing his head as Harold started to put his fingers in Rusty's mouth, the first step in preparing to file teeth—I started doubting my approach, wondering if I'd missed something by letting this horse have such strong opinions. Those strong opinions—housed in a now full-grown, healthy horse body—resulted in situations where gaining Rusty's cooperation was the only way to get anything done. Rusty had to think about things and make his decisions when he was ready. His strength was far greater than Harold's or mine. We could not force Rusty to do anything.

I'd tried to express my concern to Harold when things had

seemed a bit of a mess during a prior visit. I thought I'd used the right words in terms of being clear and understandable, but there was an edge to my emotions. My teeth were clenched as I watched what was going on. I grew increasingly uncomfortable and fought my urge to protect Rusty. What a bind. I wanted to stop the interaction between Harold and Rusty, yet I did not want to offend Harold and risk losing his willingness to come and take care of my horses' dental needs. I wanted Rusty to allow Harold to float his teeth. I wanted better communication and cooperation between these two. It never occurred to me that my apprehension was interfering with their ability to get along, alarming the ever-sensitive Rusty, and causing Harold to feel like he was being watched critically.

Years before, my veterinarian had called Rusty a prima donna. While the term prima donna has come to mean a temperamental, conceited person (its original use denoted the leading female soloist in an opera company), it can be used in a warm, loving manner. But the vet wasn't saying it that way. Rather, his exasperation was aimed at me for having a horse who needed the time he did before he'd "behave himself." This came while the vet was doing his usual annual checkup with Rusty, and watching me ask Rusty to stand or move, to lift a foot, or whatever, then wait. I did have that sort of horse—one who took his time to consider my requests. I had been practicing waiting for Rusty's readiness. Was I wrong for doing this?

Offering the choice to say yes implies that it is okay to say no as well. And as often as I've let a horse say no and then waited a bit, I've found the horse offering a yes. But this waiting for a change of mind takes time.

And that raised the question about horses behaving themselves. How can a horse behave on human terms? Most of what we ask them to do is counter to their very nature. So, in my understanding, am I enabling a disruptive, unruly horse or am I letting him be a horse as long as I'm feeling safe enough and enjoying our time together?

I also questioned why Rusty wasn't cooperative with Harold like my other horses were. I wondered if I had done something wrong. But at the time, I didn't ask myself why I felt the need to protect Rusty from this kind, competent professional. I wasn't yet aware of how my early suffocation had set me up to be scared whenever I perceived anything as containment or conflict.

I had to remember that each of us makes choices about how we handle horses. My choices reflected who I was that day and my history with life in general—not just life with horses. My reactions around horses were similar to my reactions around people. My best communication offerings around horses were similar to my best around people. I am one and the same person, regardless of what species I'm with.

That said, as so many of us know, it is often easier to be in the presence of, and communicate with, horse or dog or cat than a fellow human being. Sad, but true.

Is Anyone Listening?

"He's so naughty."

Someone was dissing a horse named Red, and I was getting upset. I was the newest employee at a therapeutic riding center near the coast of New Hampshire, and already digging deep to navigate the new relationships since I had this persistent desire to challenge some of my colleagues' horse handling beliefs and practices.

During a break between my lessons, I was watching Donna teach. She was a seasoned instructor with a confident presence, and was especially skilled with nonverbal students, including Alex, the student being led on Red by a volunteer. I started wondering about Donna's skill with nonverbal equines. Her body language and breathing patterns left me puzzled. What was making her stiffen and hold her breath as she was teaching? Was she scared? Was she frustrated?

Red was doing what he could to interpret the volunteer leader's directions. The horse leader was doing what she could to execute the instructor's directions. The two sidewalkers were doing what they could to ensure the smiling Alex stayed safely on Red's back, despite his poor muscle tone and unsteady balance. All three volunteers were doing their best walking close to Red while Donna called out her instructions from where she stood across the ring. "Walk on. Circle to the right. Change directions across the ring. Halt. Walk on."

I watched as Red kept stopping when the lesson plan called for walking. He was a mild-mannered redhead, a chunky teenaged draft pony, one of the small herd of therapy horses there. Built like a sleek hippopotamus, he was the prime choice for this very important role of carrying an unstable rider around and around the riding ring.

Nobody noticed his confusion, his inability to sort through the discrepancies between the nonverbal messages from these five people. Donna appeared upset with his stopping and encouraged the leader to pull on his lead rope and the sidewalkers to poke him. Red put his ears back against his neck, a horse's way of saying, "I don't like this."

Donna told me later that Red didn't like her and refused to do what she asked. And Red had kicked out at her. Kicking is a threatening behavior, hence unacceptable in the therapeutic riding world. Red was rapidly earning the "not good for the program" status.

I'd been a student of many things in my life, and at that time was an avid student of the horse. I had been exposed to some new ways to think about what I'd observed. I wondered if I could verbalize them in a way that allowed Red's point of view to be understood. I didn't know if I could, but my impulse to speak up on his behalf was greater than my fear of disapproval. Speaking up for those who are disempowered—not seen or heard or understood, and without power to advocate for themselves—had been my role in life, primarily in my work with children as a clinical social worker and therapeutic riding instructor.

I know that horses have preferences about who they hang out

with and have strong opinions about which other horses can be physically close. I know horses like predictability and consistency with an occasional dollop of novelty. Boredom can lead to dullness and dullness can lead to sudden surprises. And sudden surprises can show up as a startled horse who moves suddenly, orienting to assess a possible threat. All this is normal horse behavior.

What was not normal—and more importantly, not being noticed—was Red's current job stress. He had no choice about which volunteers would be handling him and would be positioned close enough to touch him during the lessons. The lessons were scheduled with the same riders, volunteers, and instructor for eight-week sessions. This made for short-term relationships within the teaching team, especially short when we think that horses can take up to six months to adjust to changes.

The volunteers did a pretty good job of adjusting to new teams, having the chance to chat with the instructor, other volunteers, and the volunteer coordinator, addressing their challenges and successes each day. Instructors had instructor meetings as well as emails and phone calls for asking questions and getting support for lesson challenges, such as the relationship dynamics with horses and volunteers. Teaching riding was not just about teaching riding—it included teamwork and collaboration.

But what about the horse? Who was supporting the horse to navigate the challenges of his job? Who was acknowledging in horsey ways all the millions of moments of success? Who was there for Red?

Red found a way to be heard using the only language he had: body language. Holding his breath, pinching his nostrils, pinning his ears, swishing his tail, lifting a hind leg were all easily observable behaviors. Not so easy to see were the more subtle communications of his mood: disinterested, distanced, reluctantly obedient, and submissive. We had a delightful pony going sour.

I had heard about Donna riding Red to help him learn his job, and how he'd kicked at her foot when she'd asked him to walk on.

After the lesson with Alex, I asked Donna what exactly had she experienced with Red? What led her to refer to him as naughty?

Donna said she increased her leg and heel pressure into his sides, and when he stood there, she started tapping his side with a riding crop to urge him to walk. That's when Red lifted a hind leg and kicked out. It sounded like a protest. Red hadn't understood what she wanted and was busy defending himself, rather than complying. He was confused and hurt. I wanted to help this go better. Better for Donna, and better for Red—the nonverbal vulnerable one.

Donna and the rest of the staff agreed to give Red a chance to change rather than find a new home for him. I offered to support Red's changes by helping staff and volunteers to listen better to what a horse might be telling us. In the subsequent training, staff and volunteers practiced new ways to pay attention to Red, who responded with a big sigh of relief. His bad reputation dissipated and he became a favored therapy horse for the years before he retired.

The Simple Cure

In contrast to Red, who was deemed "naughty," Molly was the sweetest, well-trained mare I'd ever met. She was a middle-aged, buckskin-colored mare with a college degree in walk, trot, and canter. She knew how to balance herself when carrying a rider. She was patient. She trailer-loaded and stood for the vet and for her feet to be trimmed. She was an all-round get-along-easy type of horse. But like Red, Molly was experiencing burnout, although in a different way.

Molly lived at the therapeutic riding center in Maine where I first interned and later achieved my instructor status under the guidance of the program director, herself a seasoned PATH Intl. instructor. I was the equivalent of an elementary school student as an instructor, while Molly could have earned her equine master's degree if that existed. She had more education and skill than I could use for my lessons. I got to know her when the program director, baffled by Molly's reluctance to be saddled and ridden, asked for help.

Molly had started showing signs of burnout. I suspected she needed some time off just to be a horse. I offered to take her home with me, where some herd-based R&R might refresh her spirit. We would assess what she needed after her break from the lesson barn. For some horses, time away from their work performance expectations is all they need.

Burnout shows up when a horse loses interest in relating and responding to human requests. Sometimes this type of change in a horse is due to pain or unrecognized illness. Molly was good at her job, good at doing what people wanted her to do. She was athletic enough, trained enough, healthy enough, kind enough, calm enough. But despite all this good stuff, she had started pinning her ears when being groomed and tacked. She knew that these activities preceded being ridden. More poignant was the dull look in her eyes, and her increasingly evident disinterest in being caught in the field and led to the barn. It was like every cell in her body was saying, "Oh no, not this again."

What a treat for me to have Molly at home. I didn't ride her often, but I did take her to my friend Jan's farm for a riding lesson followed by a trail ride, me on Molly in my customary blue jeans and Jan in her spiffy jodhpurs on Dudley, her retired eventing horse. It had been love at first sight for Jan, especially as Molly had a history of doing cross-country jumping—something Jan had gobs of experience with and something I had started to mess about with when she and I went trail riding together through the sandy bushland stretching out behind her little farmstead. Finding a log and cantering over it was something that I had done as a kid. Now, as an adult returning to horses, I had been finding my courage and balance to try this again on Rusty. I never rode Molly over jumps because I had an unspoken promise to honor her rest time and let her mostly just be a horse in my herd.

I was also giving her a break from being handled and ridden by a variety of people, as is the common practice at therapeutic riding programs. Some horses tolerate this well, but many do not. Horses, like people, need an adjustment period when getting to know new people and their habits, expectations, and ways of communicating what they want, like, or dislike. Keeping it simple was part of the R&R. We wanted to see if Molly's interest in people and activities would resurface.

She flourished in my herd. What a joy for me to come out in the morning at feeding time! There was Molly, standing side by side with Kacee near the rest of the horses, no longer standing off at a distance, keeping to herself. Molly grew to be curious, head low, ears forward as she moved toward me when I approached her. Horses are born with this desire to feel safe and to connect. Although human contact had dampened her interest in connecting, now it was returning.

I could have kept Molly. That was the understanding from the start. If Molly would not recover her *joie de vivre*, she could stay as mine. I was tempted to lie about her improvements. I would have loved to have her live with us forever. Sometimes I still regret my honesty. But accurate assessment of Molly and her recovery and readiness to return to the therapeutic riding program took precedence over my desire to keep her and enjoy her. That would have been a treat for me but would have nagged at me, as I am ethically committed to telling the truth. Plus, if I did have Molly to ride, I would probably spend less time with my two Morgans, Kacee and Rusty. Their training needs would suffer if I wanted them to become fairly reliable and adaptable riding horses. So, I announced Molly's likely success and recommended she have lots of time outside in a herd, just being a horse. Limit her stall time, be thoughtful about who handled her and who rode her, and keep an eye out for earliest signs of her hanging back and not wanting to engage in the human-designed activities.

And off she went, much to the happiness of the therapeutic riding center staff, and to some degree, mine as well. I felt pleased she did so well in my care, in my herd, allowed to mostly just be a horse for a few months.

Listening

When I say, "I hear you," I'm telling you I'm all ears. I am paying attention. I hear your words. I sense your mood. I am open to receiving what you are expressing even if I don't yet fully understand what you are saying. I've quieted my other thoughts and am doing my best to listen to you.

Listening and expressing and speaking are different elements of communication. Listening is primary. Developmentally, we hear long before we can speak. In the womb, we are affected by sounds we hear. We have no protective boundaries. Our entire bodies reverberate with the vibrational energy in our environment. We can be soothed by the sound of ocean waves as our mother walks on the beach, or startled as an alarm clock dings. Our reactions to sounds are invisible before we are born.

Once we're born, our eye movements and hand and arm gestures are visible, and we hope someone notices. We interact much like our horses at that age, wordlessly responding to the environment and our internal drives. We have needs but, unlike horses, we cannot mobilize to meet them. We depend on others to come when we cry, interpret our body language and vocalizations, and then take action to meet our needs.

The bodies of our horses and fellow humans are speaking all the time, and we are capable of becoming better listeners. I heard Rusty loud and clear when he swung his head away to avoid the hands of the equine floater. I interpreted his movement as self-protection—not disrespect, nor a sign of incompetence on the part of the floater.

I was trained to listen to parents, teachers, and adults in general. Listen and obey. Then I started to hear the unique inner directions that would steer me, for better or for worse, into the adventures where lessons await. This type of listening became the entryway for learning about myself, about my horses, and about the people in my life.

There's an element of *Me First* as we develop some independence from the opinions, directions, and rules of others. We listen to that inner voice and take risks to follow its quiet guidance, becoming freer and more authentic. We could spend our lives replicating the child/parent and student/teacher dynamics, or struggle to step away from the familiar roles of following, or rebelling against, another's plans. Adhering to the customs of family and culture is often easier, and relationally safer. But maybe it's not safer in the long run when the attributes that make each of us special have been sacrificed.

Feeling heard is how we develop a sense of safety, trust, and being a valued participant. It's a relief for those who have not been listened to enough, like Red. He wasn't comfortable in lessons, and how he expressed this was threatening to the people around him. He needed them to change, and they did. With Molly, nobody heard her more subtle cry for help. She needed a break from her job as a therapy horse. After her time off in an environment with few human requests, she was ready to return to work.

We all need to be heard, understood, and helped to feel better. Anybody can learn the messages of body language and be available to intervene. We can support our horses to settle after an upset and ease their return to a state of emotional balance and curiosity. All of this support flows from an attitude of doing this together; if we could verbalize the attitude to the horse, we would convey, "I'll help you as much as you need."

Without our attentive and educated presence, our domesticated horses are stressed by confinement and confusion. Understandable nonverbal interactions are the norm among horses in a herd. Not so much with human groups, or mixed-species groups of horses and humans.

The efforts we make to expand our awareness will enhance our connection and effective communication. In therapeutic and regular riding programs, we want riders, their families and caregivers, volunteers, the staff, and—of course—the horses, to all feel safe enough to be relating and learning together. It's all about how we are in relationship to these others. I promote making the conscious effort to act from our best intentions. And making the effort to stretch today's limits will develop tomorrow's better capacity.

CHAPTER 17

Be the Calm

We heal in relationship and relaxation.
— STEPHEN J. TERRELL

AM I READY TO RIDE?

IN THE PROCESS of recovering from a fall off Rusty, I decided not to ride him unless I could meet certain conditions. In fact, I wouldn't mount any horse until:

1. I start with groundwork to connect with him and see how easy it is to direct him to walk, trot, turn left and right, stop, back up, and stand still.

2. I can be present enough to notice what he can handle today and not take him anywhere (even to the other end of the arena) if he shows any concern whatsoever. When my mind is preoccupied, I cannot offer that support to both of us.

3. I can ride out *any* expressions of his worries that might happen despite precautions #1 and #2. If my physical and mental abilities are diminished, I cannot promise I'll ride those first seconds of power-burst without letting my fear reaction take over. When I'm adding fuel to the fire by grabbing with my inner thighs, holding my breath, and pulling on the reins with the hope of slowing him, I have no business riding.

I wasn't riding Rusty often while I was still healing from an injury six months prior. No broken bones, but I'd jarred my lower back and neck enough to warrant some chiropractic care, lots of ice packs, and a growing caution about re-injuring my tender joints. It was a tall order for me as a human and a rider to proceed safely and with integrity. I was certain I could not count on myself to ride through any big, worried movements Rusty might offer because I kept missing signs of his smaller worries. And my self-protective instinct was still strong. I didn't want more pain. That meant my mind was busy with worst-case scenarios, and my body was tense, ready to grasp with everything I had should my balance be threatened.

I had ridden my Morgan mare, Kacee, numerous times during those months of healing. Her worry showed itself earlier and smaller, plus I could recognize it sooner and direct her to something that felt safer than bolting. I followed the same rules for her as for Rusty but found that if I took care of #1 and #2, then #3 wouldn't arise. And if it did, her survival instinct in action was usually a straightforward gallop, which was easier to handle compared with Rusty's. He would buck and bound, as if he didn't really have his own innate safety plan. Kacee's plan was clear and distinct: Run for home. And I could ride that with confidence. My body had done it more than a few times and it had become second nature. But as I mentioned, I preferred helping her feel safe with me making our decisions before we left the ring.

Anyway, following an injury—especially a horse-scared-me-hurt-me injury—I did a ton of wondering about what I had missed. What happened before this happened? And what could I do differently to prevent any recurrences? I started to approach the whole relationship more cautiously and, at the same time, with more certainty about what I had learned and could now do differently in order to keep us connected and safe—or at least within sight of our comfort zones.

It used to be easy for me to ignore all the possible ways I could be hurt around horses. Those moments of diminished awareness or full-scale forgetfulness were the moments that left me vulnerable. My main job became developing a clear sense of whether I could stay in my best mindful and aware state while riding. I knew how to ride. I had adequate technique about horses and riding under my belt. It was this other stuff that I now wanted to grow and expand, for the rest of my life. And in my desire for a *long and active* rest of my life, I would stay with my feet on the ground with a horse until I was feeling confident we were connected—not just that the horse was doing what I asked, but that the horse and I were tuned to the same wavelength. I want to know the horse is feeling open to my leadership presence and looking for my direction—not just accepting it or, worse, just tolerating it or bracing against it.

My baseline of what a calm, ready horse looks like and feels like kept changing as my awareness grew.

After my injury, I was riding less. The more tenuous connection between my mind and my body left me cautious when I was hurting. My body was not as strong or agile as it would be after my injuries healed. My instincts to protect myself were stronger than my intent to behave as the most considerate rider I could be. I could not offer a calm state when I was worried about my wounds. So, I was on the ground for the most part and learning, learning, learning as I interacted, paid attention, and interacted some more.

SINGING

I have a good enough voice to be singing in public. I was once a backup singer, harmonizing with singer/songwriter Azaima Anderson at a New Year's Eve gig in Portland, Maine. And I was a member of Next Voice, an all-women a cappella group which performed in one of Portland's public parks. But this background doesn't really matter—I do not actually need to have a good singing voice for some occasions.

Like the day I remembered that singing is good for calming and cadence when riding a horse. I remembered this while astride Rusty, flanked by the yellows of daffodils and forsythia bushes on our first trail ride of the spring season. We had left some riding buddies a few miles down the road, and we were headed home alone, just Rusty and me. And Rusty was neither calm nor proceeding with a regular cadence.

Not before I started singing, that is.

I've been working on the railroad, all my live long days...

Huh? Where did that come from?

Someone's in the kitchen with Di-nah.

Someone's in the kitchen, I know-o-o-o...

Ah, yes. I'm starting to understand. I can easily sing these songs in tempo with Rusty's walking stride. And when I slow down my singing a little? He slows his walk a little. I was not going to test this too much in case our success was a fluke. I don't want to lose the good thing we've suddenly got going.

Then "Jingle Bells" comes bouncing out of my mouth. Lively song! Lively Rusty!

Oh, no! Quick! Change the tune!

How about a lullaby? Let me think...

Lullaby, and good night, la lala laaaa, la la laaaa.

That was effective.

Then back to *Someone's in the Kitchen with Dinah* because I like singing the *fee, fie, fiddle-e-i-o* parts.

I am truly amazed by how singing affected our ride. Past the snapping white wire tape near the strawberry fields. Rusty yawning and sighing. Past the kids playing ball and the bright yellow mailbox that has always been cause to stop and gape. Ho-hum. Okay, I exaggerate about the mailbox, but he did keep walking without any completely frozen moments, just lost track of our musical harmony for a few strides.

I may never perform again at a New Year's Eve festival. I may never again join a group of women singing a cappella African chants and four-part gospel harmonies. But I do have a musical future. One that will make a difference where it really counts. It will make a difference to my horses.

Just Say Yes! to singing with your horses!

Falling Off

I loved almost everything about teaching. Except when someone got hurt.

Cathy was lying on the ground, frozen on a hot summer day. She was stunned, unable to piece together what had happened. Eyes open but unfocused, speechless, chest heaving. Slowly taking in where she was and what had happened. Nobody knew yet if she was okay. My focus was on her as I hurried across the ring, not noticing my own fear yet, busy searching my memory for the emergency protocol for falls. *Clear the ring. Call for help. Don't move the person. Check for breathing, responsiveness, body parts appearing out of place, blood.* I was holding my breath as I looked for her breath. She was breathing. I breathed, and hints of my own frantic and terrified undercurrent started to surface. Crises freaked me out. I urgently wanted another adult staff member to walk through this with me.

Cathy was a shy teen and a keen horse enthusiast, with a history of learning disabilities, social anxieties, and awkwardness not uncommon for traumatized youngsters. This was Cathy's first fall from a horse. As her instructor, I was responsible for the crisis response decisions. My training and my job description put me in charge at a time when I really didn't want to be in charge. I was ready to phone Cathy's emergency contact person, but uncertain whether to call the emergency response team, likely a legacy from my own early trauma. *Does she need more help? She's breathing so she must be okay.* Seeing the site coordinator walking toward us brought relief. She would know what to do thanks to her well-developed sense of priorities, plus prior experiences with students falling off horses. Her taking charge let me bring my best skill set forward: ease with being present with people as they come out of shock.

Fear shows up when riders fall off horses even within the highly regulated, safety-oriented lessons in a therapeutic riding program. Fear impacts the riders before, during, and after falls. It impacts the volunteers who take pride in helping the lessons be safe for our riders. Fear impacts me as the instructor watching a student lose balance, fall, and experience the impact as body meets ground. And yes, fear impacts the horses, too.

The best scenario for our riders falling off is if they are small-bodied, start very slowly to lose their balance, and have two sidewalkers ready to catch them in the moments between losing balance and landing on the ground. I've witnessed some fine acrobatics by sidewalkers softening a fall by catching a rider in their arms, or assisting the rider to land gently, feet first. My breath caught when watching Cathy, an independent rider without sidewalkers or horse leader, lose balance in the middle of a lesson and fall, landing on her back with an audible thump.

Shock at a fall permeates every member of the team, including me.

Sometimes this shock is from the rattling of bones and tissue as the body tumbles onto the ground unexpectedly. Sometimes it's from an experience of moving too fast to register what happened, much less integrate it. The sudden changes of orientation, direction, and speed are only part of what the brain tries to keep track of as we are moving through space. Cathy and her horse had been moving together in a certain direction. Cathy sat at a certain height from the ground with a plan for where they were going and at what speed. When her horse sped up, she wasn't able to adjust and go faster, too. Her body got stiff thanks to the fear response, and in the discombobulation that ensued, she and her horse parted ways. Something to keep note of for the future: A rider who has enough skills to ride independently may not have enough physiological capacity to shift quickly with the horse. Horses are superb at shifting quickly. We humans, not so superb.

I was in my element being with Cathy as these discrepant experiences started to connect, as her senses and nervous system started having a reunion as she lay there on the ground. Breathing, verbally responsive, blinking, making eye contact, wiggling her fingers and toes. She was remembering where she was and what had happened. So far so good. No broken bones. No broken skin. Helmet in place. Starting to test her extremities and following my direction to *not* move her head and neck. She reported some ache in her left knee. That was it for now. No emotion showing up yet, nor the shaking that wants to happen despite being trained from an early age: *Don't shake. Don't cry. Here, take this medicine to inhibit the normal behaviors that accompany coming out of shock.*

Meanwhile, our executive director, with her perfect mix of caring heart and decisive presence, had called the first responders. We had previously had meetings and discussions with local first responders, asking them to arrive without lights flashing or emergency vehicle sirens that would further upset people and horses. So, they came quietly, assessed quietly, and pronounced Cathy okay enough to get up and go on with her day.

Some horse people insist that the first thing you do after falling off a horse is to get back on. I am not one of those horse people. I won't even offer that as a possibility. No getting back on before there's plenty of time for the after-effects of shock to show up and be experienced, then settled. Shock itself is designed to numb us from pain and/or fear. It's a balm—though a temporary balm. When you are deep in the analgesic of shock, it is not the time to resume riding.

I love teaching what to do after a fall. My protocol? The fallen person is to be still, assess from the inside, reach out verbally for help, and accept the comforting presence of someone calm and well. There needs to be someone in the dedicated role of simply being a calm, caring, and protective presence. Let the others take action, call for emergency response, clear the area, whatever is needed. But one person needs to be there simply to be calm and attend to the person who fell. This calm presence is what allows the scared, shook-up person to start letting down from the physiological fear and shock response.

If this designated calm person is missing at the time of the fall, the regulation can happen later. Think of the child who is hurt and doesn't cry until Mom shows up. Sometimes this regulated support never happens, and the person goes through life with unresolved shock and a braced stance, limiting how life is experienced. The emotions, sensations, and memory details of the fall and the landing remain locked inside. The changes that happened too quickly to be registered become the overwhelm stuck in a rider's body, interfering with movement, attention, and adaptability.

That is my other professional expertise, that of a trauma resolution specialist.

Be the Calm

We are social animals. We need the calming presence of another's nervous system before we can move toward regulation from an acute or chronic dysregulated state. We cannot develop this capacity to shift in a relational vacuum.

Family members, friends, animals, even strangers can help us settle through co-regulation. Likewise, we can be the calm for others. Co-regulation doesn't require talking about what happened or even knowing what happened. Words aren't needed, and at times can be an impediment to settling. In order to be our best, we are called to excavate our unconscious and befriend whatever is hidden under layers of adaptive protective defenses. Those defenses intrude into today's relationships again and again.

Human infants and horses of any age are similar, having no boundaries to insulate themselves from the energy of others' emotional and physiological states. This is helpful when we are in proximity to benevolence, but disruptive when we are exposed to dysregulation.

When I'm disoriented like Cathy was after she fell, *pausing* opens the door for me to feel inside, while someone witnesses and accepts me as I am. Then, like ripples in a pond, the waves of disturbance spread out, and a quieter version of me reappears.

The sequence for assisting nervous system shifts starts with *Me First*. As flight attendants remind us, when we fly with a child and the oxygen masks drop, we must first put on our own and then attend to the child. Same with horses: first look to our own settling and then look to helping the horse. In other words, if I'm wound up, I can't help my horse settle.

What if we can't easily return to a sense of connectedness—accessible in the calm of our parasympathetic state—after an upset? We use management strategies that will shift us toward a calmer state. I can check my breathing. If I'm holding my breath, I start breathing. If I'm breathing in a shallow and rapid manner, I slow it down, with an emphasis on breathing into my lower torso and extending my exhale—even blowing air out slowly for as long as I can. This alone communicates to both my own brain and to people and horses around me: *I am feeling safe enough to breathe slowly and deeply, so you can feel safe, too.* To become more grounded, I can bring my attention to feeling the ground me. These are a couple of easy ways to help our horses settle. Settling myself means they can settle.

Other activities help, such as swaying, hopping, and hugging. My singing while riding Rusty helped us to stay connected and feel safe enough together. There's meditating, creating with art, music, or words, sipping tea, and napping. And soaking in a hot bath, walking in the woods, planting a garden, or pausing in a quiet place free from the concerns of pleasing others, meeting others' needs, or questioning if our hair looks okay and socks match. What might work for you?

We use management strategies like these when we lack the ingredients—unpressured time in a safe environment—that allow the waves of activation to come to completion on their own. After the waves complete, we need fewer strategies for shifting states; the completed waves change our state from the inside.

From 2020 to 2022, we were in a state of inescapable threat due to COVID-19 and the scary news reports. This global menace left no one immune. Most everyone on the planet felt unsafe and lived in relentless high sympathetic activation. In 2022, add the war in Ukraine to the increasingly publicized political divisiveness. It is exhausting to be on alert all the time. Unsustainable. What do our nervous systems do when we are threatened and our reserves are depleted, whether we like it or not? Take the express lane into an immobilized state, slamming on the brakes while the accelerator is still fully engaged. But even this shut-down state saps our life energy.

We hope we will emerge again, however messy that will be.

If a virus can mutate to survive, we can, too. Instead of a genetic transformation, maybe it will be a social-relational mutation where new responses to danger or threat replace habitual fight/flight/freeze/collapse responses. This could help us survive and feel safe with others. We could eliminate what threats we can and coexist with the threats we cannot.

We have moments of relief when we pause and feel a hint of aliveness, connection, and hope. This experience, even if it is brief, is essential. Rest and connection prepare us to surf the next waves of sympathetic activation.

If we want our horses to be in a learning frame of mind, we can help them by bringing calmness and clarity to every interaction, whether the horses are calm or not.

I am devoted to becoming more dependable and consistent, and a better support to my horses. I have them in my life because I want us to get along and enjoy our time together. If I am well regulated, we have a better chance to do things together. If my horses are well regulated, it feels like a gift. The more consistent and regulated I am, the easier it is for us to get along together.

Epilogue

We're all imperfect beings making our way through life.
— KARA L. STEWART

With all the messy stuff, no matter how messy it is, just start where you are—not tomorrow, not later, not yesterday when you were feeling better—but now. Start now, just as you are. — PEMA CHÖDRÖN

FIXING THE GUTTER

TERRY AND I hauled a couple of eight-foot ladders, a cordless drill, a box of screws, and a long piece of pipe to the run-in shed where our horses, Rusty (now twenty-five years old) and Sam (twelve), were eating hay. It was starting to get dark, and we were determined to make a new drainage route for the rainwater that runs off the roof into the gutter. To prevent more flooding in the run-in meant getting this done before the rain that was supposed to start the next morning.

About the time we climbed the ladders and started installing the length of plastic drainpipe, Rusty and Sam stopped eating and wandered over. The horses were as calm as they were curious, and stepped close to sniff the ladders and touch them with their muzzles, their way of getting to know something new. I suspected they might also investigate the ladders by nudging them, and we didn't want that. We didn't want to be tipped over. I climbed down and said hello, reaching out to scratch Rusty along the underside of his neck. I wanted to lure Rusty and Sam out to the nearby field where they'd graze and leave us alone to finish our project.

I started walking and Rusty came with me, his head near my right shoulder. This position made sense. He had gone blind in his right eye, so he could keep track of me better by using his left eye. And even with one eye blind, or maybe because of this, he was showing his trust by coming along as I walked.

Rusty had been not only aging, but aging with illnesses. He lost the sight in his right eye from uveitis. He breathed with great effort. He'd been diagnosed with chronic obstructive pulmonary disease (COPD), often called heaves in horses because of the way they breathe. Some days, I could hear Rusty breathe from a distance. Most days his breathing was mildly labored, more visible than audible. He inhaled, then pushed out his exhalation. He had lost his ability to chew hay easily. His molars—designed to grind hay—were worn smooth. He rolled his hay rather than ground it. The solution for that was feeding him soaked hay cubes, which I did, three or four times a day.

I cried often, holding anticipatory grief in one hand and here-and-now adoration for this amazing animal in the other. Me, with my sweet sorrow as his health declines. Rusty, with his mix of feisty and opinionated and gentle, despite his age and ailments.

I realized Rusty was becoming dependent on me. This shook me up. I had avoided dependent relationships for most of my life. When I was young, it felt unsafe to depend on others. My personal healing allowed me to accept Rusty's growing dependency. This was sweet. That sweetness that comes with sorrow and decline at the end of life. That sweetness that deepens the ties between two beings, despite impending loss. I discovered it was possible to welcome dependency.

I was becoming better because of my efforts to be a better horse person for Rusty.

Dear Rusty

Dear Rusty,

I adored you from the start. Adoration isn't always the best basis for a long relationship. But it was our start. That and the deep bond cemented when I saved your life. I found you upside down, a yearling, cast in a stall, months before I committed to owning you.

Yet you scared me and puzzled me. You needed things from me I didn't know how to give. I wanted to be better for you—kinder, more knowledgeable, more skilled, able to make choices based on wisdom, not fear or tradition. I wanted to get along with you. I needed to unlearn as much as I've had to learn. Remember when I tried to hug you when you were a youngster? There I was, sad and lonely, leaning into you for comfort. But it troubled you. Penny and Kacee and other horses had been okay with my hugging, but not you. I have had to make efforts to be who you needed me to be.

Many teachers helped me understand you. Many teachers and therapists helped me understand myself. I learned to be with my old hurts, to hold them gently as I wanted to be held. This freed me from expecting you to be my blankie, my big warm snuggly. I had to uncover and release hidden traumatic memories—especially of being suffocated by someone bigger than me—to be a better person and a better horse owner. Thank you, Rusty, for tolerating my learning curve. For not killing me.

Even though I've so desperately wanted you and other horses to be a calm, wise presence for me, I've become the grown-up in our relationship, the regulated one who offers guidance you understand. I've learned to turn to people when I need help to feel safe and to settle. Coming to you when I am upset is unfair, and I don't want to be unfair to you. I know better now and can tell when coming close is harmonious.

I've kept you in captivity in the best way I can, giving you free access to things you need: shelter, food and water, space—and most importantly—to horse company. I'm sorry for your distress in these years since Kacee died. In our smaller herd now, you have had less choice about who will be your buddy. I know you've not really gotten along with other horses like you did with Kacee. I miss her, too. I wish she were still alive and here with us. I imagine something inside you would feel really good if she were still here, like the world would be a safe place again.

I'm still unlearning the notion from my past that I'm the authority in our relationship. I'm hopeful but awkward as I explore a more consensual relationship with you. I don't give you choice when it's time for veterinary care, but I give you choice about what I can. I wait for your readiness to lift a foot when I want to clean your hooves, I wait for your readiness to be haltered and led to the barn, to stand still when I saddle you. I regret all my pushy behaviors and frustrations I've directed at you: blaming you when I'm scared or when you've not done what I've asked, resenting the care you've needed this past year. It's mostly a cover for my deep sorrow when I think about how your declining health has limited your quality of life in these days.

When I'm scared or angry, I have learned to make sure you are safe and then walk away until my strong emotions settle. I know you need the calm version of me. I don't want to repeat those experiences when I couldn't offer you my patience and courage, when feeling abandoned quickly turned to you taking care of yourself as if I wasn't there. And at times, I wasn't actually there in spirit.

Our time together has helped me get to know when I'm present with you and when I'm not. I am grateful for learning about myself, unraveling the hidden motivators, and having second chances to show up without the ghosts of the past disturbing our relationship.

Everything both you and I do is for a good reason, even though I may not know what that reason is. There's an element of survival interlaced everywhere, from the survival need of being in a herd to the survival need to run scared when a threat is perceived. What's been so messy is when you are scared and then I get angry because your fear and your behaviors scare me. You have hurt me. You have kicked me. You have stepped on my toes. You have bucked in such a way that I've lost my balance and fallen to the ground. And in my limited abilities and my own self-protective habits, I get mad at you when you are the perceived threat to my life.

This commitment for a lifetime thing has been hard for me. I've been influenced by the tradition, "For better, for worse, for richer, for poorer, in sickness and in health." Right now, I'm referring to my commitment to you, Rusty. But I'm also talking about my commitment to my partner, to my dog, to myself. Suddenly we are all getting older and running into more health complications at the same time.

You and I, Rusty, have been robust and vibrant. Until recently, I have not had concerns about your health. I had assumed your wellness would continue until the day you would die. But now I do have concerns about your health—more than mine. I still identify myself as remarkably healthy, especially for someone my age. Interestingly for both of us, our lungs are our weak point. I wish I could fix your lungs so you wouldn't cough as much as you do. Some might say it bothers me more than it bothers you. I know it bothers me, but I don't know how much it bothers you.

Deep inside, I know my only choice is to adapt and adjust and try out more health-enhancing possibilities for both of us. Experience reminds me I can tap deep into my belly for that extra strength to go through the steps of another day with a sick horse, a sick dog, a sick partner, and worries about my own health.

I'm doing the best I can, Rusty, being brave, taking risks, guessing at your needs, consulting with professionals and trauma-informed horse-owning friends. I hope it's enough. I hope you are comfortable.

Thanks to the clarity of your requests, I am becoming better at listening with my observing eyes, my breath, my gut feelings.

I want to do the right thing for you and for all the horses I meet. You all have helped me so much. I'm grateful for the kindness of all who have helped me become a better version of myself.

This is for you, Babe. I'm glad you are alive. And I hope this book benefits other horses who live and work with us humans.

Love,

Me

Sample Exercises

*I wish I would have known more back then. I know
I can't start over but I can change the ending.*
—M. Wylde Williams

You must do the things you think you cannot do.
— Eleanor Roosevelt

Here are three sample exercises from my next book, *Cultivating Connections: Experiential Exercises for Home and Horse Barn*. I love problem solving and adapting exercises to specific situations, so please contact me with questions, comments, or requests to create custom exercises for your situation.

Rocking to Balance

1. Stand or sit comfortably and feel your weightiness, how gravity draws your body toward the earth. If sitting, notice if your weight down through your pelvis feels the same on the right side as on the left side. If standing, notice if your weight down through your pelvis to your feet feels the same on your right as on your left.
2. Start rocking gently from side to side, just a small rocking motion.
3. Slowly decrease the range of your rocking until you find a middle-balanced place.

4. Pause and feel what this is like.
5. Lean to the right a little, using a hand on something for stability if needed.
6. Pause and feel what this is like.
7. Lean a little more to the right until you feel the edge of coming off balance, then come back to the middle.
8. Pause and notice what's happening with your energy, breathing, heart rate, sense of contact with the earth/ground.
9. Lean to the left a little, using a hand on something for stability if needed.
10. Pause and feel what this is like.
11. Lean a little more to the left until you feel the edge of coming off balance, then come back to the middle.
12. Pause and notice what's happening with your energy, breathing, heart rate, sense of contact with the earth/ground.
13. Be curious about where you:
    - feel wobbly in each direction.
    - are more stable.
    - tense up more to prevent falling over.
    - hold your breath.
    - relax and release your breath.

You now have an enhanced sense of balance.

Story Time

1. Sit comfortably with your favorite writing tools, such as computer, paper and pen, pencil, or colored markers—and a timer.
2. Envision something about a horse or horses.
3. Start the timer and write for ten minutes.
4. Read what you have written and underline the adjectives and descriptive phrases, whatever sticks out as you are reading.
5. Write your name at the top of a separate page, then list all that you underlined.
6. Consider that these words and phrases describe you.

7. Read this list of descriptives silently or out loud.
8. Notice your responses: emotions, thoughts, sensations.
9. Option: Draw an image that represents your story.

You have gained some insights while creating a story.

Feeling Our Boundaries

1. Invite someone to be your practice partner. Choose who will move first and who will stand still first.
2. Stand about twenty feet apart, facing each other, in silence if you can.
3. As the mover, start toward your partner and stop when you first notice you're feeling "too close."
4. Ask yourself: What am I feeling, sensing, thinking? What do I want to do now?
5. Back up one step and assess again. Back up or move forward until you find the distance that feels just right.
6. Pause in the just-right spot.
7. Discuss what you noticed with your partner, then switch roles.
8. Extra challenge: Do this with a practice partner as above, but while leading your horse, walking alongside a friend, or with your dog on a leash. Your challenge will be to find the distance that feels "just right" for you *and* your horse, friend, or dog. To do this, you will be noticing and honoring your own responses as you did above, and at the same time, as best you can, the responses of your horse, friend, or dog.

You have just increased your awareness of the internal changes you experience when you approach someone, while tracking your own sensations and also paying attention to your companion's responses.

Gratitude

How wonderful it is that no one has to wait,
but can start right now to gradually change the world!
— ANNE FRANK

AT DIFFERENT TIMES in my life, I have been happily dependent on family and friends as I stretched into learning new things. I give thanks to those who shaped me as a person, shaped my commitment to writing, and shaped the development and birth of this book.

For my therapeutic riding career, I give thanks to the therapeutic riding professionals who drew me in and nurtured my involvement: Stephanie Keene, Barbara Doughty, Sarah Armentrout, Heather Bagley, Liz Claud, and Nicole Jorgensen. Thanks to the riders and their families for trusting me with some of their horse education and granting permission for me to represent moments from our lessons. And special thanks to the many staff members, volunteers, and horses I had the privilege to work with.

For my clinical development, I give thanks to Daniel A. Hughes, PhD (attachment), the late Sandra Cummings, RNCS (psychodynamic), Peter A. Levine, PhD (and the array of Somatic Experiencing® trauma resolution faculty and assistants), Dave Berger, MFT, PT, LCMHC (BASE™), Katherine Allen, LMFT (Brainspotting™), Stephen Terrell, PsyD (attachment and Transforming Touch®), and Sarah Schlote, MA, RP, CCC, SEP (Equusoma®).

I give thanks to the horses I've owned, enjoyed, and learned about relationships with. My Copper Penny, Fairlane Kacee, and Fairlane Rusty are the three Morgan horses most prominent in my heart.

Of course, thanks to my (now deceased) parents, Sonia Lasell Jaretzki and Alfred Jaretzki III, and to their parents and our ancestors who instilled in us a love of horses along with access to them, with generosity and assistance on many levels. They also passed along a love of words, books, and the great outdoors.

And thanks to my circle of friends who have cared for me with listening, reading, and encouraging my writing and my personal evolution: Bhasha Leonard, Sarah Schlote, Lyra Halprin, Karen Baril, David Solomon, and others whom I hope will forgive me for not specifically naming them. Thanks to the *many* additional horse and psychotherapy professionals who influenced my horsemanship and my trauma-informed skills.

Thanks to the professionals who have helped birth me as a writer: Anna Blake and Crissi McDonald of Lilith House Press, Catherine Parnell and MaxieJane Frazier of Birch Bark Editing, and Janna Maron and Karen Beattie of More to the Story. And to my editorial team: Bhasha Leonard, MaxieJane Frazier, Kate Washington, Jonah Meyer, Madhuri Z K Akin, and Sarah Schlote; and my designer, Gopa Campbell. Their encouragement and orientation to detail made it seem easy to prepare this book for publication. And deep gratitude for the option to self-publish under the supportive umbrella of Crissi McDonald's and Anna Blake's Lilith House Press.

I give thanks to all the humans and horses who have offered me their curiosity and trust over the years and have led me to pause and wonder and learn new things.

And last but by no means least, I thank my beloved Terry Sweitzer, and our animals—you keep teaching me more about love and commitment and belonging than I ever could have imagined.

PATH International

PATH INTL. WAS formed in 1969 as the North American Riding for the Handicapped Association to promote equine-assisted services (EAS) for individuals with special needs. Since that time, the association's work to credential professionals and accredit centers has expanded, as have the categories of individuals served by EAS. Through the work of 813 member centers and more than 5,424 professionals credentialed through PATH Intl., 53,399 children and adults, including more than 5,900 veterans, find a sense of health, wellness, a sense of independence and fun through EAS. Member centers range from small, one-person programs to large operations with several credentialed instructors and licensed therapists. In addition to horseback riding, a center may offer any number of EAS such as hippotherapy, carriage driving, interactive vaulting, trail riding, competition and more. Through a wide variety of educational resources, the association helps individuals start and maintain successful programs. There are 49,705 volunteers, 6,781 equines and thousands of contributors from all over the world making a difference in people's lives.

MISSION STATEMENT

We lead the advancement of professional equine-assisted services by supporting our members and stakeholders through rigorously developed standards, credentialing and education.

Vision Statement

To ensure universal recognition of professional equine-assisted services and their transformative impacts that enrich lives.

References

Grateful acknowledgement is made to the following for the use of quotes in *Getting Along with Rusty*, listed in order of appearance in the book:

Page vii
Printed with permission from Harry Whitney. *Harry Whitney–Horsemanship . . . from the horse's point of view*. https://harrywhitney.com.

Page 3
Goodall, Jane. "Jane Goodall Hopecast #16: From Japan to Tanzania, Jane Listens to Hopecaster Messages of Unity and Action for the Future," *Jane Goodall's Good for All News*. June 8, 2021. https://news.janegoodall.org/2021/06/08/jane-goodall-hopecast-podcast-final-episode-season-1-mailbag/2/.

Page 9
Printed with permission from the *Rumi Network*. https://www.rumi.net/rumi_poems_main.htm.

Page 17
Estes, Clarissa Pinkola. "You Were Made For This" by Clarissa Pinkola Estes." *AWAKIN.ORG*, January 28, 2008. https://www.awakin.org/v2/read/view.php?tid=548.

PAGE 31

Nagoski, PhD, Emily, and Amelia Nagoski, DMA. *Burnout: The Secret to Unlocking the Stress Cycle*. New York: Ballantine Books, 2019, p. 27.

PAGE 41

Tatkin, Stan. *Wired for Love: How Understanding Your Partner's Brain Can Help You Defuse Conflicts and Spark Intimacy*. Oakland, CA: New Harbinger, 2012, p. 21.

PAGE 57

Dana, Deb. *The Polyvagal Theory in Therapy: Engaging the Rhythm of Regulation*. New York: W.W. Norton & Company, 2018, p. xvii.

PAGE 67

Schlote, Sarah. *Horse-Human Trauma Recovery: A Polyvagal Lens for Equine Interaction Programs* [draft manuscript]. Guelph, ON: EQUUSOMA®, 2019, p. 187.

Nagoski, PhD, Emily, and Amelia Nagoski, DMA. *Burnout: The Secret to Unlocking the Stress Cycle*. New York: Ballantine Books, 2019, p. 80.

PAGE 81

King, Lily. *Writers and Lovers: A Novel*. New York: Grove Press, 2020, p. 151. Kindle edition.

Porges, Stephen. "Courses." *Polyvagal Institute*. https://www.polyvagalinstitute.org/courses-1.

PAGE 95

Brown, Brené. "Brené Brown: 3 Ways to Set Boundaries." *Oprah.com*, August 20, 2013. https://oprah.com/spirit/how-to-set-boundaries-brene-browns-advice.

Schlote, Sarah. "Safe Haven Relationality." *EQUUSOMA® Horse-Human Trauma Recovery*, accessed March 22, 2023. https://equusoma.com/about/approach.

REFERENCES

PAGE 109
Drucker, Peter. Interview with Bill Moyers: *Peter Drucker: Father of Modern Management*, November 17, 1988. https://billmoyers.com/content/peter-drucker.

PAGE 121
Printed with permission from Anna Blake. *Anna Blake, Author, Horse Advocate & Trainer.* https://annablake.com.
Merton, Thomas, and Naomi Burton. *The Asian Journal of Thomas Merton.* New York: New Directions Books, 1975, p. 308.

PAGE 133
Printed with permission from Crissi McDonald. *Crissi McDonald, Heartline Horse Training.* https://crissimcdonald.com.

PAGE 145
Oliver, Mary. *Devotions: Selected Poems of Mary Oliver*, New York: Penguin Books, 2017, p. 264.

PAGE 157
Dass, Ram. "Being Love." *Ram Dass Love Serve Remember Foundation.* https://ramdass.org/being-love.

PAGE 159
Printed with permission from Leslie Desmond. *The Feel of a Horse.* https://feelofahorse.com.

PAGE 175
Maté, Gabor. Foreword to *In an Unspoken Voice: How the Body Releases Trauma and Restores Goodness*, by Peter A. Levine, xii. Berkeley, CA: North Atlantic Books, 2010.

PAGE 185
Keller, Helen. *We Bereaved.* New York: Leslie Fulenwider, Inc., 1929. https://archive.org/stream/webereavedoohele/webereavedoohele_djvu.txt.

PAGE 197

Printed with permission from Gail Ivey. *Gail Ivey School of Horsemanship*. https://www.gailivey.com.

PAGE 211

Printed with permission from Stephen J. Terrell, PsyD. *Austin Attachment and Counseling Center*. https://austinattach.com.

PAGE 221

Adapted with permission from Stewart, Kara L., *Fall Down Seven Times, Stand Up Eight*. Grover Beach, CA: Blue Imaginarium Press, 2023, p. 212.

Chödrön, Pema, and Emily Hilburn Sell. *Comfortable with Uncertainty: 108 Teachings*. Boston, MA: Shambhala Publications, Inc., 2002, p. 90.

PAGE 227

Adapted with permission from M. Wylde Williams. https://www.facebook.com/photo/?fbid=688520713274526&set=a.471164105010189.

Roosevelt, Eleanor. *You Learn by Living: Eleven Keys for a More Fulfilling Life*. Louisville, KY: Harper & Brothers, 1960, p. 30.

PAGE 231

Frank, Anne. *Anne Frank's Tales from the Secret Annex*. Translated by Susan Mossotty. New York: Bantam Books, 2003. First published 1983 by Washington Square Press, p. 225.

PAGE 233

Professional Association for Therapeutic Horsemanship International (PATH Intl.) https://pathintl.org/publications/2022-fact-sheet.

About the Author

It's our nature to get along.

LASELL JARETZKI BARTLETT, MSW integrates over fifty years of experience in the fields of bodymind awareness and meditation with professional expertise as a Clinical Social Worker and a PATH Intl. Therapeutic Riding Instructor and Equine Specialist in Mental Health and Learning. In private practice, she facilitates trauma resolution from early childhood trauma, falls, medical trauma, and meditation dissociations, helping people develop a sense of safety that can support the best relationships imaginable. To enhance her professional offerings, Bartlett became a practitioner of Somatic Experiencing®, Bodywork and Somatic Education™, Brainspotting™, Somatic Resilience and Regulation®, and Transforming Touch®. In addition to assisting regional, national, and international Somatic Experiencing® and Equusoma® trainings, she has presented on trauma healing at conferences for mental health and therapeutic riding professionals.

Her writings have been published in *The Natural Horse Magazine*, Mark Rashid's *A Journey to Softness*, *What She Wrote: An Anthology of Women's Voices*, *We Had To Be: An Anthology by Breast Cancer Survivors, Previvors, Thrivers, & their Families*, *MicroLit Almanac*, and *Osho News*.

Bartlett lives on a small farm in rural Virginia with two horses, seven sheep, three donkeys, seventeen goats, thirty guineas, two cats, three dogs, and her bestest ever human friend.

Printed in Great Britain
by Amazon